KAYAK THE MYSTIC WATERS

*Sea Kayaking Journeys in Southeastern
Connecticut and Rhode Island*

Joseph F. Taylor

PINE POINT PRESS

Published and distributed by Pine Point Press,
Mystic, Connecticut
Orders for this book should be directed to:
www.kayakmysticwaters.com
www.pinepointpress.com
pinepointpress@aol.com

All photographs and charts by the author.

Library of Congress Control Number: 2006939580

ISBN-13: 978-0-9790419-0-7

ISBN-10: 0-9790419-0-2

Front Cover Photograph: *The Mystic River Drawbridge from
the water.*

To my wife and best friend, Karen.

Chart Legend

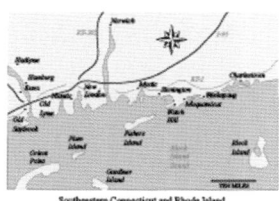

Southeastern Connecticut and Rhode Island

Major Roads

Minor Roads

Railway Bridges

Compass pointing North

Contents

Acknowledgements

I would like to thank my wife Karen and my close friend and fellow paddler John Pattenden for their thoughtful input as this book was being compiled. I am forever grateful to the Tuesday Night Paddlers (especially Marty Young, Bill Morrison and Stan Bowdish) for organizing wonderful kayaking itineraries over many years. I have drawn generously on these itineraries in writing this book. Thanks also to Marty and Bill for kindly reviewing a late draft.

The photographs were taken with three different cameras; a SIGMA SA-7 film SLR, a Kodak CX7530 digital using an EWA Marine waterproof bag and a Nikon Coolpix 8800 digital. I will be happy to acknowledge kayakers who are shown in photos (and send them copies!) if they contact me.

The charts were drawn on a Wacom Intuos-3 digital pad using a variety of sources (including MAPQUEST). These charts are for illustrative purposes and are not intended for precise navigation. The reader should consult NOAA charts for definitive navigation aids.

The inspiration for the front cover was from the book *River Days* by Michael Tougias.

The timeless river classic *Three Men in a Boat,* by Jerome K. Jerome (the first travel book that I ever read), was in my thoughts as I wrote this book.

<u>About the author</u>
Joe Taylor is from Ireland and has lived in Mystic since the late eighties. He can be contacted with questions/comments at pinepointpress@aol.com.

This is intended to be a lighthearted book and not to be taken too seriously. The information presented will hopefully be helpful and informative to the reader. All water sports carry inherent risks of injury or death. While the author believes the kayaking information in this book to be reasonably accurate, he is not a professional instructor or navigator. The author cannot be held responsible for the safety on the water of those who use this volume as a reference.

List of Charts

7

Chapter Ten: Fishers Island

Chapter Eleven: Further Afield

Introduction

This is a little book about kayaking in Southeastern Connecticut, particularly in the Groton, Stonington and Fishers Island area. I am not from around these parts, but I've lived in Mystic for seventeen years now. Through kayaking, I've come to see this as my own place because there is a certain strip of coastline here that I know like the back of my hand.

The steamboat Sabino on the Mystic River.

When I was growing up, we had to make our own entertainment. My family was quite poor, but we did not realize it since everyone else was the same. We never really went on vacations or the like. In the long summer holidays from school and at most other times of the year as well, I rambled the roads and fields near home with my cousin and a couple of other friends. When you are walking, you see so many things, the gaps in the hedges and walls, what the crops are like in the fields, whether the road is flat or has a slight incline. You see a bit less on a bicycle (although you certainly are more aware of any incline!), less again on a motorbike, and least of all in a car. In this regard, kayaking is like walking; you see everything there is to be seen, and you

"Friendly" swans building a nest on the river.

can stop and look at anything you want to. All you need is water that is a few inches in depth so that you can hug the coastline and see the waterfowl, the grasses and the waterside homes.

A lot of my most enjoyable kayaking involves just moseying around, going with the flow, and enjoying the sights. One of my best friends, John, is from England, and we have kayaked together here for a good couple of years now.

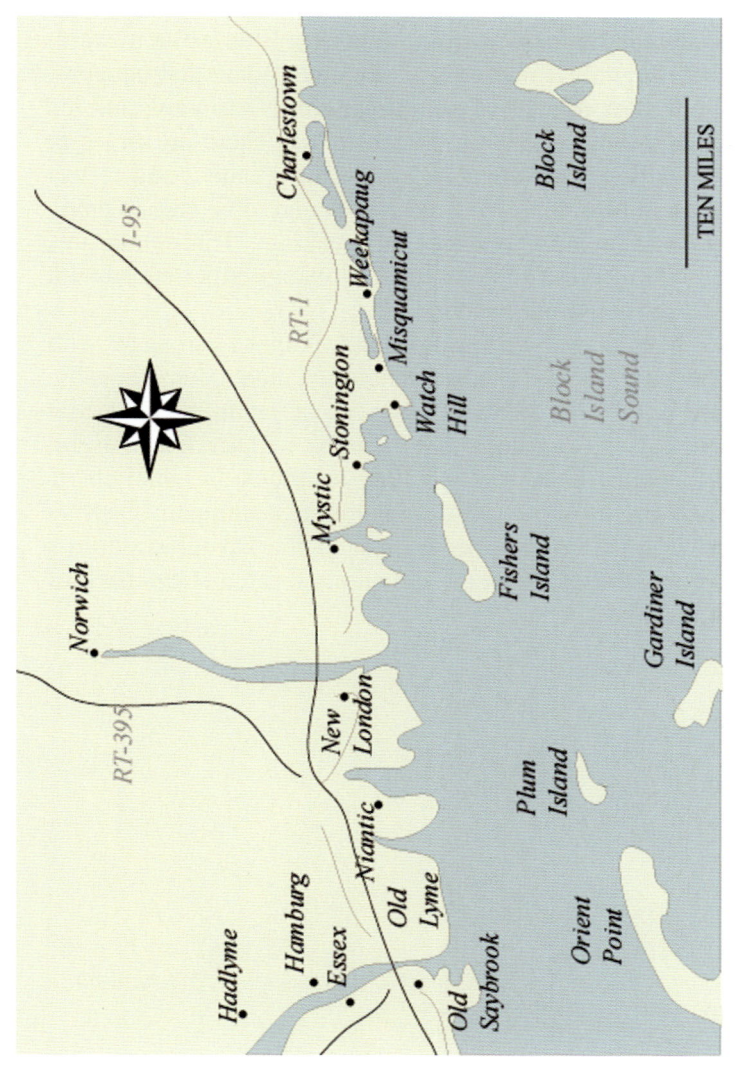

Southeastern Connecticut and Rhode Island

13

If John has a fault it's that he likes to talk. It's a funny thing but when I mention this to my wife, Karen, she tends to look at *me* and give a little cynical chuckle. When John and I are kayaking together or in a group, it takes a little while to warm up properly and get into a good rhythm. When that happens, on a good day, mind, body and boat are in harmony, and the conversation and good stories can flow. There are times in every paddling year when we are in the moment and reflect on our good fortune to have our health and to be able to enjoy the lovely, simple experiences of kayaking. Throughout this book, I will mention some of these moments experienced with John, Karen and other friends.

My hope in writing this book is that I can share with you the enjoyment, beauty, tranquility, and companionship that are to be experienced while kayaking in Southeastern Connecticut. Also, I hope that the book will serve as a useful guide to some of our best paddling locations. Original charts and photographs of the areas being toured accompany each chapter. You can also locate most of the kayaking put-in's that are mentioned, from the directions located at the back of the book.

1

The Mystic River

(Kayaking guide to the Mystic River. War of 1812. Mystic Village and Seaport.)

The town of Mystic is my center of gravity for kayaking in this area. The river here is very picturesque, and it also provides easy access to Fishers Island Sound and the surrounding coastline. There are plenty of good put-in's for paddlers on the river. On the Groton side, north of Interstate 95, near the Daniel Packer Inn at Fort Rachel or on the Stonington side, off the Mystic Community Center beach (MCC, now the Y) near where I usually launch. As you depart from the beach to go downriver, you pass Masons Island on your left, the south part of which is a gated community. The gates are referred to locally as the "pearly gates" probably because it's easier to get into heaven than pass through here. Just recently, a sixteen hundreds Indian grave was discovered on the north side of the island while excavating for a house foundation. Reportedly, there were up to sixty remains all facing east in the traditional burial manner of the Mashantucket Pequot Indian tribe.

The Mystic River has a very rich past. In the little known war of 1812, Mystic was one of the ports blockaded by the British navy. Apparently, the locals were so troublesome to the Brits, venturing out in sailboats at night to attack their ships; that Mystic was dubbed "that hornets' nest"! Another cute story from these times concerns forays that British marines made up the river to attack the "hornets' nest", in open longboats on both occasions. The first attempt, in the dark of night, they rowed up the wrong channel and found themselves stuck fast in the mud on the south side of Masons Island. They had to wait there for the incoming tide to free them, praying, no doubt, that they would not be discovered in the interim. On the second attempt, again at night, they found the river, but as they passed Pine Point, the scrape of their oars in the oarlocks carried easily across the river to what is now Fort Rachel. This "fort," just south of the current railroad bridge, is distinguished by a house-size rock on a property then owned by a woman called Rachel, hence the name. Local defenders were keeping watch on a make-do structure on the rock and heard the noise of the oars. They discharged a small cannon in the general direction of the longboat, and this was enough for the Brits to turn tail. This war reads like two kids boxing each other without either trying too hard to land a punch for fear that it will turn into a real fight. Not that there's anything wrong with that!

***

So, enough history for now. As you leave the Mystic Y, with marinas on your left, you head past Pine Point. Just before the point, there is a little cove with sea grasses and pleasant summer homes to peek at. Staying on the Stonington side of the river, you will pass Masons Island Marina and little Abigail Island. A couple of years back, I brought a friend, Joe, out kayaking for his first time. He was doing pretty good as we paused near Abigail Island for a breather. There was a good tidal current flowing past, and Joe got mixed up between the island and the current; and I heard a splash and "glug, glug

The Mystic River

glug" behind me. I surmised correctly that he had gone for an unexpected dip. No matter, he clambered ashore and recovered his dignity. Here the river opens wide with the island on your left and wetlands and verdant grasses to the right. Once you are out of the main channel, you can easily find shallow water to paddle lazily and relax out of reach of most boats.

I should say that the Mystic River is very busy with power and sailboats in the summer. Also, you will nearly always bump into other kayakers. It's a pleasure to paddle along and watch the assortment of boats pass by. You will see motor yachts up to one hundred feet, little sunfish and day sailers and everything in between. On the whole, everyone is friendly and courteous. It always warms my heart how people salute each other on the water.

A couple of hundred yards farther to Ram Point, which has a unique, multilevel brown-colored wooden home with a glass or Perspex dome. The little beach here is a good place to rest or look for shells. From there, I usually head on a line to Morgan Point Lighthouse. In season, this takes me through various mooring fields with probably over a hundred sailboats. I entertain myself by checking out the boats and looking for any that are on sale and within my price range. It is a very pleasant and harmless pastime once you don't make the mistake of actually buying a boat. This way, you can do it every year with no resultant financial damage. One day, last summer, I went downriver on a very foggy morning. It was like visiting a totally different place. In the mooring field, you could only see one or two boats at a time, the rest hidden, mysteriously in the fog until you came upon them.

Morgan Point is a beautiful lighthouse. The light itself, now defunct, sits atop a sturdy granite building to which an elegant grey-shingled home is attached with green lawns running down to the river. The house was featured in *Coastal Homes* at Christmas, a number of years back. I often worry whether people who live in such beautiful, luxurious surroundings are really happy, but my wife assures me that they are!

You meet all sorts on the river. One day, near the lighthouse, in early spring, the water still very cold, I stopped to chat with an older man who was coming in from the Sound. He immediately volunteered that he had open-heart surgery some months previously. Almost in the same breath, he offered that he had just kayaked out and back to Fishers Island, a six-mile haul!

***

From Morgan Point, the sea kayaker has many options; continue west to Esker Point and Groton Long Point, the demanding run to West Harbor in Fishers Island, around Ram Island or farther east to circumnavigate Masons Island. If you turn to go back upriver, you will pass marinas and colorful Noank on your left. There are several riverside seafood shacks to visit here, Costello's, which is a typical clam shack and Abbot's, famous for lobster in the rough, eaten outdoors. Noank village itself is a delightful maze of lanes and quaint New England homes. Well worth a ramble. You can pull in at the little village dock and explore.

As you proceed upriver, you should take the time to glide into Beebe Cove. It's hidden in behind the railway line and is accessed via a little archway under the tracks. The town of Groton has a recreation center on the banks of the cove with rowing shells and sculling lessons available for residents. When you reach Ram Point, check out the wetland grasses on your left again. Near Pine Point, you will see the Mystic Yachting Center on your left. This building has just recently been leased to a local sailing club. On a Sunday in mid-October, I watched a fleet of their JY 15's race in the inner harbor. The wind was gusting up to forty knots, and the boats were screaming across the water. A friend of mine was a participant, and he not only capsized several times; but his mast got stuck in the mud and broke! He and others have suggested that I might join the club, but I demurred!

International scullers near the Mystic River Drawbridge

Moving on, you head for the Amtrak railroad bridge. The bridge is always opening and closing for the New York–Boston trains, but you need not concern yourself about this. As you paddle up towards Mystic, you will be flanked on each side by sailboats and motor cruisers at dock. If you fancy refreshments, try the Daniel Packer Inn just nearby the local water-access ramp. On the Stonington side, just below the Route 1 bridge, the townspeople have constructed a beautiful *pau-lope* boardwalk with a green lawn beside it for concerts and entertainment. There are public restrooms here if you need them. Last year, there was a two-day rowing event on this stretch of river, and I motored up in a small inflatable to see it from the water. Some of the U.S. Olympic team participated in the event, and it was very exciting to watch and chat to the racers.

The Mystic Bridge itself is a bit of a treat. It is a rather rare, original working bascule drawbridge. It has enormous concrete weights perched on high, which serve as counterbalances to "see-saw" the steel road-structure up, allowing boats to pass underneath. It opens hourly, in season, to allow boats upriver. "Type A" boaters and (and motorists!) can get very frustrated at the antics of this bridge. Sometimes it opens and doesn't close; sometimes it closes and won't reopen. For some reason, kayakers never seem to get upset by all of this; we just glide along underneath it all! If you want to stroll through Mystic, just beach your kayak nearby, and you will be downtown in a jiffy. The Town of Groton has just recently installed a floating dock for kayakers, just by the bridge! If you have an hour or two to spare, go visit the Mystic-Noank Library on the hill. It's a delightful old building with great nooks and crannies in which to read peacefully. The village also has a couple of good ice-cream parlors, several pub-restaurants, and lots of little colorful shops. Well worth a visit.

Near the bridge, you may see several river, cruise-boats docked. The *Valiant* is a new aluminum-hulled replica of a large 1920's classic power yacht. It is rented for parties and weddings and has a rich, wood-paneled salon. North of the bridge, there are a couple of traditional schooners, the *Argia* and the *Mystic Whaler*, that offer half-day cruises. This is a great way to see the river and Fishers Island Sound if you don't have a boat.

We are now heading up toward the Mystic Seaport. On your left is Captains Row. This is a riverside road heading out from Mystic, lined with traditional sea-captains homes. It can also be cycled or walked, along the river, all the way to Old Mystic, and the tranquility and peacefulness here are well worth the couple of hours of your time. Across from Captains Row is the Mystic Seaport, a world-renown, seafaring museum and village with many relics of Mystic's whaling past. There are many interesting features here for visitors. Another riverboat, the *Sabino*, is docked there. It's an original, coal-fired passenger steamboat that tours the river regularly in season. Again, it's a great way to see the sights.

You will remember the deckhand shoveling coal into the furnace below and the distinctive "toot toot" of the *Sabino*'s whistle, which is familiar to everyone on the river. It's nice to see it chugging along as you paddle. I also love to glide

John, kayaking at the Mystic seaport.

slowly by the large black whaling ships that are permanently docked at the seaport. If you visit, it's also worth checking out the marine art gallery and store.

Perhaps the biggest annual event on the river is the antique boat parade, which is hosted by the seaport. Scores of classic boats, mainly wooden, from near and afar parade "through" Mystic, downriver to Morgan Point and back. Many of the craft are decked out as party boats for the day with young men and women dressed in twenties period costumes. It is just delightful to paddle with and through the fleet as it wends its way along. The event also draws hordes of colorful kayaking groups, so there are plentiful opportunities to stop and chat and exchange stories.

From the Seaport, you can continue north to Old Mystic passing under the highway bridge. The river is quieter up here, and it always feels like a long pull to me, although it can't be much more than a mile. As you return, you may want to stay near the coast by the railroad bridge and as you head back to the Mystic Y beach. It's always interesting to peek at the shore, the homes, and the grasses.

2

Masons Island

(Indian graves. Tour the island. Strange mishaps. Masons Island Yacht Club. Enders Island, a precious jewel. Pogy Bay.)

Masons Island is about a third of a mile wide and a mile long and sits in the estuary of the Mystic River. Legend has it that before the English settlers arrived in the region, the local Pequot Indians would come to the island each summer to fish, clam and eat wild berries. Apparently, they would burn all of the bushes on the island once each year to ensure strong regrowth and a plentiful supply of fruit. By all accounts, the Pequots were a rowdy, warlike bunch. When the British came to the area in the sixteen hundreds, there were many schamozles initiated by the Pequots against the Crown soldiers, at least that is the history that I have heard. As in all wars, the victors tend to write the script that is handed down. The British eventually lost their patience and, in the Battle of Fort Hill, massacred a large portion of the tribe and scattered the rest to the four winds. Major John Mason was awarded what is now called

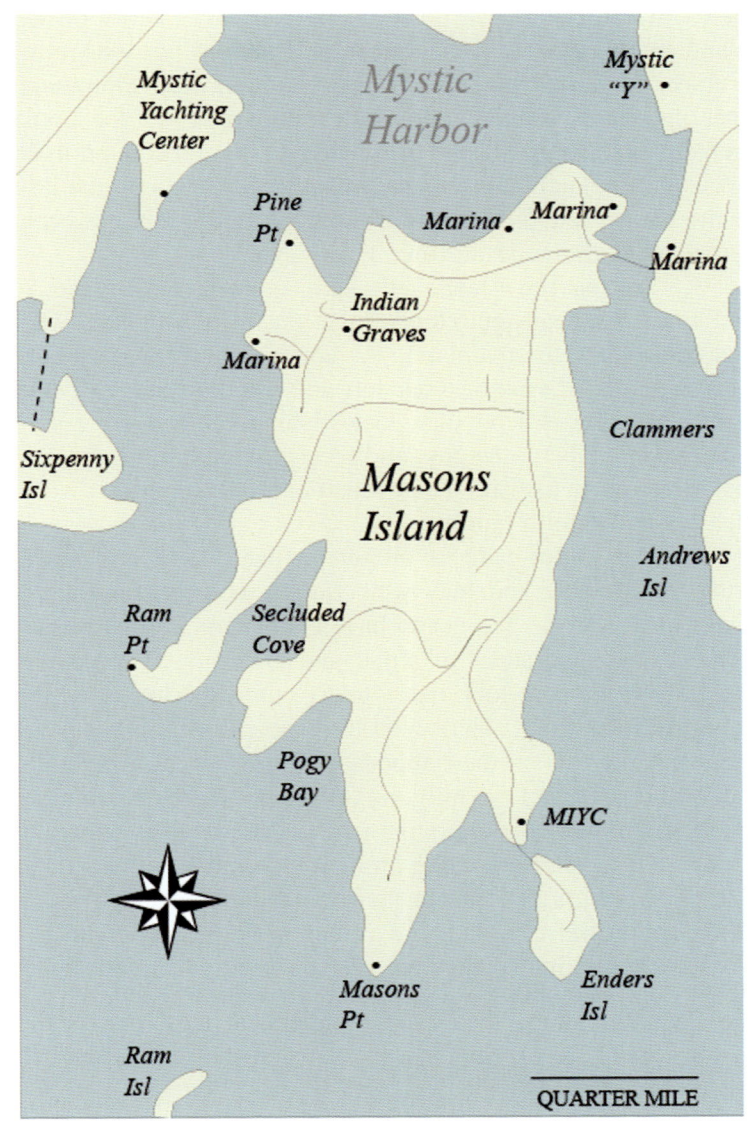

Masons Island

Masons Island, and other local lands as a reward for leading the Crown forces. There is a very informative history of the island by James Allyn the father of Rufus Allyn who now oversees the gated community and has significant dominion over the entire island. Some interesting facts in the book include; that John Mason is reputed to have been born in Norwich, England, and died in Norwich, Connecticut; the last of the Mason line died in 1940, and an Allyn family has been associated with the island since 1776.

To tour the island, let's start again at the Mystic Y and, this time, head south toward the Masons Island causeway that connects to the mainland. As you paddle along, you will pass Schafers Marina on your left and a trailer park on your right. Schafers is a popular, local fishing center. They rent small open boats by the day, and locals take full advantage of this opportunity to fish. The owners and operators are a very pleasant and helpful family.

The trailer park is an interesting oddity. It looks pretty ramshackle and may well violate most of the zoning codes in the book. It's got to have twenty trailers in various shapes, sizes, and states of repair and disrepair. The people that inhabit the park look like a pretty contented lot. It really is highly frustrating. Here, you have people who can't have spent much at all on their abodes, living cheek by jowl with those who have laid out millions for the privilege of living on the island. The really annoying part is when you pass by and see Ozzie and Harriett sitting on their stoop, the grill sizzling, a beer or a glass of wine in their hand, looking much more relaxed and carefree than some of their well heeled neighbors. To add insult to injury, they are very pleasant when you salute them, returning your "It's a nice day." with "Ah, its grand altogether." It always unsettles me going by that area.
Abutting the trailer park is another little marina.

A strange story unfolded there a couple of years ago. I think it was in December on a cold and stormy Sunday. The account told is that two men who lived together, year-round, on a small cabin cruiser, decided, out of curiosity, to take a runabout down to the mouth of the river to see what the conditions were like. Sometime later, a cook and a kitchen helper on Enders Island (Enders is at the south end of Masons Island) were outside smoking a cigarette by the seawall. They heard someone shouting for assistance and discovered one of the men on the rocks on the other side of the wall. The story that the survivor related (as I heard it, at least) was that the boat's engine ran out of gas at the mouth of the river, and they drifted four or five hundred yards offshore. For some insane reason, both men, wearing life jackets, decided to jump into the sea and swim for shore rather than stay with the boat. One of them swam to Enders, and the other's body was not found for a week or so. He eventually drifted ashore in Block Island about twenty-five miles away, sans life jacket!

There have been several other strange mishaps in this area in the last couple of years. One is an infamous case of a schoolteacher kidnapped by a friend of her husband. She escaped and made it home only to be found dead at the bottom of the stairs two days later. Then, there was the case of a young man who left a local hostelry late one evening to motor back to his boat in an inflatable. Next day, his body was found washed up on the island and the inflatable elsewhere. I also heard a recent account of a young woman who fell off a rock into a pond on the island and drowned. I am not a superstitious person, so I assume that these are chance occurrences rather than a cluster of ill fortune associated with the island.

***

The Masons Island causeway is immediately beyond the trailer park and marinas. Up until 1912, there was no bridge as such, and the island was accessible only at low tide via a cow track. The bridge under the causeway cannot be more than ten feet wide, and there is a fast current flowing through it when the tides are running. You generally want to hit it in the middle and with a bit of speed if you are going against the tide. About ten years ago, the Community Center had a couple of rowing sculls for use by its members. I tried to scull through the archway under the causeway once in one of the sculls and got badly caught up with the sidewalls. Thankfully, I just drifted back out of it with the tidal flow. This little bridge is a very popular spot with local anglers, young and old. It is very common if you are driving over the bridge to see fish breaking on both sides. Give a holler to the anglers to avoid getting hooked as you pass underneath.

The water opens up into a broad shallow estuary on the other side, and you will see a lot of families clamming here in the season. I had never seen how clammers operate until I came to this region, and it was quite a surprise to me. In essence, they walk along in the water often submerged up to their necks; sometimes gaiters or wetsuits are worn, sometimes not. The clams are collected with custom-built rakes that are used to scrape the muck on the bottom and sieve out the mollusks. A common way of holding the clams while collecting is in a net draped through an inflated inner auto tube, the net and shells immersed in the water. Often whole families work together and use small inflatable boats to store their catch. It's very interesting and colorful to see the carry-on on a good day.

You have the option here of heading east toward Latimer Point, but today we will keep on track to circumnavigate the island. Staying by the shore, you will see a variety of coastal homes, some grand, all desirable. It's not unusual to see families swimming off of their docks. This side of the island is a little monotonous from the water although the views from the shore are stunning. As you come toward the south end, you get a panoramic view of Fishers Island Sound and Latimer Light. On your right is Masons Island Yacht Club. This is a private club, and you must live within the pearly gates to be a member. There are active sailing events at this club. The kids do the dingy thing, and there is also a fleet of one-design Shields that race weekly.

***

At the tip of Masons Island is another small island called Enders. These two are connected via another causeway. This island is a precious jewel. It is no more than a quarter of a mile long. At the beginning of the twentieth century, it was settled by the Enders family who built a stone mansion on it with beautiful gardens, walkways, and bowers. When the last of the Enders, Alys, passed away in 1954, she bequeathed the island to the Society of St. Edmund, a Catholic religious order based in Vermont. The island is still in the hands of the Edmunites today.

In my jogging years, I would sometimes run from the Mystic Community Center to Enders and back but had never gotten to know what was out there. One Sunday morning, in December, I wandered out to the island and entered the old church to say a prayer. Mass, in fact, was in progress, and my relationship with Enders had begun. This church is a small modest building, probably fifty years old. It has space enough for a small congregation, and the priest and the community were very close to each other there.

Over the years since, I have attended church at Enders and made a couple of very good friends. One of these was Charlie Conway. Charlie was in his early seventies when I first met him, a tall, bearded, barrel-chested man. He was a kind, soft-spoken person who loved to sail and brought me out on his sloop a number of times. In the couple of years that I knew him, he took several interesting trips. One year, he booked a passage aboard a freighter and traveled to many parts of the world as a paying passenger. Another dream he had was to travel up the Hudson to Lake Erie. So, that year, he bought an old motor cruiser and headed upriver. He came home once to recharge and ended his trip when Lake Erie's

29

waters were too rough. The following year, he died suddenly in his sleep from a heart attack. While I miss his company, I feel good for Charlie that he followed his dreams in those last few years.

The small Enders community is very welcoming to visitors. They also run various retreats, and it's a great place to visit if you just want to rest and think. The community built a new stone chapel on the island a couple of years back. It is a beautiful building which fits in well with its surroundings. It has great wooden trusses and beams inside, and multi-colored stained glass windows that illuminate the body of the church when the sun shines.

The alpine oratory and new chapel on Enders Island, photographed from the rocks.

As you approach Enders, you have the choice of going through the causeway or around the island. This causeway is similar to the last, a couple of hundred yards long with a small bridge in the middle. If you are driving to church, there is room for just one car to pass at a time. The waters under this bridge can have even faster currents than the previous one as it is more exposed. When you go through, there is a good stretch of open water until you reach the next tip of Masons Island (Masons Point). If you decide instead to paddle round Enders, you will see a small, striking outdoor oratory on your right. It is alpine in style and is really just a little space with an opening toward the sea. People place various offerings on a stone slab against the back wall; medals, prayer cards, shells, and the like. It gives it a very voodoo'ish feel, which is added to by the darkness and dankness of the place. The oratory is built on a long flat ledge that slopes into the sea just thirty feet away. It's hard to convey the feel of the place in writing, but it's a very spiritual spot especially when standing on the rocks looking out to sea.

A little bit beyond here, the island is protected by a massive, ten-foot-high seawall that was constructed after the hurricane of 1938. This hurricane was a defining event in Southeastern Connecticut and Rhode Island. Over four hundred people were killed in the devastation it brought with it. A neighbor of mine, Bill, was a child attending school in Mystic at the time. He tells the story that the storm hit as he was making his way home from school. To avoid being swept away, he would grasp at telegraph poles, and the force of the wind gusts would lift him horizontally as he clung on for his life. He recounts that the storm surge was twenty feet high at Enders, and the resulting spray drenched Mystic two miles away. Hence, the wall, which cost a million dollars to build in 1940.

***

You won't see that much more of Enders as you head west back toward Masons Island. There is a low bungalow built on the tip of the island here. It's set well back from the water, which makes sense. Sadly, it seems to be used only in the summer, which is a bit of a shame, given the beauty of the location. Weather conditions need to be considered if you decide to paddle around the island. The seas can be quite challenging at this spot as you round the rocky point. I've occasionally found myself paddling very hard and carefully here to make meager progress into a strong headwind and broadside seas.

If you are in a hurry, you can paddle directly across to Ram Point from here. But if you are out for a nice day or couple of hours, take the time to hug the shore and explore little Pogy Bay (come to think of it, "Hug the Shore" would be another great title for a kayaking book). This coastline is very rocky, and these same rocks serve as foundations for several of the houses. One group of cottages sits right on the ledge, and to swim off the rocks here must be delightful. A little farther on, there is another swimming area with a very small beach that families use in the summer. It's worthwhile paddling into the very end of Pogy Bay to experience it fully. The first time I visited here, I was overcome by the simple beauty and calm of the place and envied the children who grow up and mess about in such idyllic surroundings.

Still staying by the coast as you leave the bay, you will have the choice to go through or skirt various small reefs. My decision, invariably, is to play in the shallows. That's the beauty of a kayak; you can glide in amongst submerged rocks with only a couple of inches of water depth. The worst that will happen is that you will get stuck and need to back out (although it is easy to tip over if you hit something unexpectedly). There are various groups of underwater rocks in and around Pogy Bay, and I keep hitting a particular one in my sailboat. A neighbor of mine says that the only rock you really know is the one you hit, so I'm hopeful that my luck will improve. Also here to your right, beyond Pogy Bay, is a beautiful long inlet with wondrous waving grasses to explore. It is unexpectedly deep and winding and the last turn brings you close to a beautiful waterside home. You don't often see anyone in here, and it is very quiet.

Finally, you reach the Mystic River. As you pass

Pine Point, upriver, take the time to glide into the little cove just beyond it. This is the location of the Indian graves that I mentioned earlier. They were discovered during an excavation for a new home. The owner of the land and the Pequots quickly came to an agreement allowing the tribe to carry out an archeological excavation. The graves were laid down at different times during the sixteen hundreds as evidenced by black layers of soil, which are remnants of bark that was used to line the base of each tier. I have heard a couple of stories as to why the graves are located here. The

A quiet cove nearby the Indian graves on Masons Island.

one that appealed to me the most is also the least likely to be true. This holds that the Pequots had a camp in nearby Noank and canoed across the river to bury their dead at Pine Point, nearby, but not too near. As an ardent kayaker, I felt that this story connects us to these long-departed souls. The likely true history, recounted by tribal historians and archeologists, is no less poignant. After the massacre at Fort Hill and the granting of the island to John Mason, Pequot Indians worked as slaves for Mason and lived and died on the island. Contrary to my idyllic version, it was their custom to bury their dead nearby their camp. Rufus Allyn is permitting the tribe to survey adjoining land for remnants of a campsite. They were buried here with all of their worldly possessions, cups, beads, and the like.

3

Getting Started

(Purchasing a kayak. Contentious rudders. Beginner lessons. Keeping it simple.)

I was introduced to kayaking by a friend who owned two kayaks at the time (Old Town types), and I think we went out in them at least once. As I began to show a little bit of interest, she told me about an open house at Collinsville Canoe and Kayak near West Hartford. She and I motored up there one Saturday, and I ended up buying my first boat.

Since that day, I have a bit of a soft spot for the Collinsville outfit. It's a barn of a place in a big car park on the banks of the Farmington River. The day we visited, they had scores of boats, new and used, on display in the car park and demos and lessons on the river. I don't know this river well, but near the kayak shop, it forms a sheltered lake with a weir upriver and sandbanks below. After wandering around aimlessly for a while, I eventually took a boat out for a paddle. I can't remember much about it other than that it was red and felt quite tippy, which got the wind up me a fair bit! Later on,

I tried a second boat, a gray polypropylene Perception Carolina, and I ended up buying that for about seven hundred dollars. This is a relatively wide sea kayak (about twenty four inches) with a rudder, and it felt very comfortable and steady. Back at the store, I added paddles, flotation jacket, spray skirt, and a temporary roof rack to bring the boat back home. The reason I liked the Collinsville outfit, by the way, is its location and setup but also because, at that time at least, it was run by a married couple with young kids and had a friendly, family-business feel to it. I was living in a ground-floor apartment in an old school building in Mystic at the time, and when I got home, I lugged the sixteen-and-a-half-foot boat through the hallways and into my living room to store it! It felt good, the beginning of an exciting adventure. I had no idea how rich an experience it would be.

A year later, I bought a second boat, again at Collinsville, a red Looksha IV from Necky. I justified this purchase as a means of getting friends and family on the water with me, which has at least partially been the case. This is my main boat now. It looks great, and I really like it.

That's how I got going. If you are interested in heading down the same road, I will make some suggestions for your benefit based on my experience. My comments will be aimed at the average recreational sea kayaker not the advanced paddler.

Let's start with filthy lucre. I have a theory regarding modern sports equipment, which I call the "thousand-dollar rule." Nowadays, it seems to cost a minimum of about one thousand dollars to get going in any sport. It's as if the sports-equipment companies have formed a cartel and decided that this is the minimum they will accept from a beginner. If it's tennis, they make up the sum from the racket, shoes, clothes, accessories, etc. Golf, of course, is a no-brainer for them. I would bet that if you decided to get serious about tiddley-winks you would discover that the serious players are using handcrafted sets, thumb bands, eye protection, scorecards and

Two sea kayaks by the floating dock near the Mystic River Drawbridge.

the like, the cost of which mysteriously adds up to a thousand bucks. The good news about kayaking is that you can get going for this amount or less. If you are on a tight budget, you may be able to pick up a used sea kayak, in good condition, for less than five hundred dollars and add the rest of the essential gear for another two hundred. Given that this will get you on the water, in reasonable safety, in spectacular surroundings, it's a real deal.

I favor a polypropylene, i.e., plastic, boat. They are considerably less expensive than fiberglass or Kevlar craft and very durable. Although a little heavier, you can drag them over sand and rocks for years without doing any great damage. Given where I live and paddle, I favor a sit-in, sea kayak with a rudder. Sea kayaks tend to be longer boats, mine are sixteen to seventeen feet, so that they can ride the waves better.

The question of the rudder is a contentious one. The purists argue that you don't need a rudder, that it slows you down, etc. Don't believe them! I tried my first boat with the rudder up for a while (to keep things simple) and came to the definite conclusion that I had been sold a lemon. It kept veering off track due to tides and wind. Even when I paddled two or three times more on one side than the other, I could not keep it on course. I became convinced that the boat had been molded badly and was fundamentally unbalanced. One day, on a whim, I dropped the rudder, and my whole outlook changed. Now, I could effortlessly go anywhere I wanted and easily stay balanced and on track. It was like night and day. In fairness to the connoisseurs, there is a definite skill to steering a boat with your body. Counter intuitively, you lean away from the direction you wish to turn. Also, a skeg or shallow keel is a big help in getting a boat to track well. Nevertheless, if you are a beginner and want to enjoy yourself and improve your skills, get a boat with a rudder. Time enough later on to try paddling without it.

The other essentials to getting started are paddles and a flotation vest. It's worth getting a decent paddle; this is the business end of the whole affair, after all. I have a pair of Werners, which I find pretty good. Recently I tried a more modern carbon fiber set, which are lighter and probably more efficient. I would recommend either of these. Obviously, you

Paddlers on "sit-ons" at the Antique Boat Parade
(not to mention the dog!).

have no business going on the water without a decent flotation vest. I have a couple of older ones, which do me quite nicely although they are a bit heavy in the high summer. Whenever I wear these out, I'll switch to the lighter styles, which are popular now. You should wear a flotation vest even when the water has warmed up since there is always the danger of banging your head if you fall in, and the buoyancy will keep you upright as you recover your equilibrium. Although not indispensable, I usually wear a spray skirt, which keeps out the waves and splashes. This is a must if you plan on a lot of sea kayaking. Karen has taken a strong dislike to wearing a spray-skirt because of the enclosed feeling, possibly because a spider crawled up her calf the first time we paddled together. Women are a little funny like that.

***

I should say, in passing, that my red Looksha is like a second skin to me now. It is hard to remember when this was not the case. There is a wonderful familiarity when I set it down on a ramp or beach, pull up the spray skirt, don the flotation vest, push the boat out a little, slide in, and secure the skirt, not forgetting the paddle. It's got something to do with the snugness of the boat and the closeness of the water.

In getting started in any sport, there is always the question of lessons and training. I come from the school that treats lessons as an afterthought, something to consider when you are a couple of years into the endeavor. The downside of this approach is obvious, slow progress, bad habits developed, etc. There are positives, however, learning with friends, learning by doing and figuring out if it's something you like before you overinvest. I can, however, recommend some inexpensive training resources. Books and videos on kayaking can be found easily in sports shops or on the Web. The major kayak retailers offer free hands-on seminars once or twice a year when they have open houses to sell boats. Also, the local kayak groups and clubs organize skill-improvement sessions a couple of times a year. In our area, these groups include ConnYak, RICKA, and the Tuesday Night Paddlers (more of the Paddlers, later). In addition to these resources, John and I and another friend, Stuart, have taken several courses at the Wickford Kayak Center, and these I highly recommend. The Wickford Center is a serious, highly professional training organization, as well as a flourishing retail outlet. Their syllabus is very comprehensive, ranging from beginner to expert skills. The topics I have covered with them include bracing (I still don't fully get this), wet exits (falling in the water), wet reentry (getting back in the boat), rescue, towing, etc., very worthwhile if you plan to spend a lot of time on the water. Another positive (kayaking) development for the region is that the giant, outdoor sports cooperative, REI, is opening a store in Cranston RI in the spring of 2007. I'm looking forward to checking out their kayaks and training resources!

I photographed this kayaker on the Atlantic coastal drive near Newport. He had just caught a big striper in the ocean.

On the subject of gear, again, there are several other items, which you may want to acquire as time goes by, some sooner than others. High on the list should be a hand pump to bail the boat if it's flooded, an inflatable float to help with wet reentries, and a line or tether for towing. I carry a sponge in the webbing to dry the inside of the boat before or after a trip and to remove any creepy-crawlies. Boat dollies are very useful for conveying your kayak a distance. I find the ones that are designed to hold the boat in position without straps the handiest. I bought one of these at North Cove Outfitters in Old Saybrook, and I would not know what to do without it now. (North Cove is another excellent store to purchase kayaks and all other accessories. They also have open house twice a year where you can try out boats on the water and also have a full syllabus of training courses.)

I have a small compass clamped on the deck just in front of the cockpit. This is very useful if fog comes in as you are paddling. This happened to me just recently. I was no more than a hundred yards from the shore, near Quiambaug Cove. It was a misty day but visibility was a couple of hundred yards. Because of this I made sure to stay close to the shore. However, I did not notice a very heavy, thick bank of fog drift in and suddenly I could hardly see beyond ten yards! You have to experience something like this to appreciate how quickly you can become disoriented. I thought I still knew where the shore was and quickly began paddling in that direction, but I did not see the outline of the coast as soon as I expected. After a while I got worried and came to the conclusion that, somehow, I had gotten turned around. I then decided to listen to the sound of traffic from Route One, which was only five hundred yards away, and head in *that* direction. Again, I paddled quite a while without seeing land. At this stage, I was getting worried. If I was not going toward the land then where was I heading for? Out to sea? And, how far out was I. Would I be stuck out here for hours, getting further and further away from the safety of land. At one stage, I unexpectedly came upon a small rock with an egret perched on it. For some reason, I took a lot of comfort from this, I was not totally alone out here. I actually said hello to the egret to calm my nervousness! Finally, I did the obvious. I checked my compass and paddled north since land had to be in that direction. In a few short minutes I spied the very welcome sight of the rocky shore, maybe twenty yards away from where this little saga began. Although I felt pretty foolish, I was very happy to hug the shore and head for home and think about the valuable lessons I had learned.

A dry-bag is very useful for storing valuables and food. John and Stuart also gave me a thoughtful gift of a handheld GPS for my wedding a couple of years ago. Karen had two comments when we opened the package. The first was "what the heck is this?" and the second was "I'm not writing the thank you card!"

I've seen several other accessories on boats in the water. Occasionally, you see a jury-rigged mast and sail, which seems like fun when the wind blows but a bit complicated. I have been known to carry a small fishing rod in the webbing on my boat. Someone asked me recently whether I fish from my kayak, and I answered quite truthfully that I do. Unfortunately, they had the bad manners to then ask if I had ever caught a fish from my kayak, and for some reason I admitted the truth rather than lie through my teeth like a real old salt. I'll know better next time. Bottles of water, sodas, and munchies are always needed. I tend to take an apple or a couple of bananas in my dry bag in case I get peckish. Cell phones and VHS radios are very useful communication tools. Lights are a must if you kayak by night.

However, to circle back to my original advice, you should not think that you need all of this gear to get started. You don't, and it will probably confuse you as a beginner. Start with a solid, inexpensive, preferably used sea kayak; a decent paddle and a flotation vest; and spray skirt. Get on the water in a sheltered area and enjoy yourself. The rest will take care of itself in its own good time.

4

East to Stonington Harbor

(Twenty-mile paddle. Coastal gentrification. Latimer fog. Stonington Harbor. Devastating fires. Portuguese fishermen. Battle of Stonington. Wadawadnack Club. Wamphassuc mansions. Thunderheads. Ram Island.)

Now, we will begin to venture beyond the Mystic River, heading east toward Stonington Borough; passing Latimer Point, Lords Point, and Wamphassuc Point; and visiting Ram Island on our way back. The total distance here can vary from ten to twenty miles depending on where you wander. This would make a good full or half-day paddle with judicious stops for rest, sightseeing, and refreshments. Alternatively, you can split it up into smaller more manageable chunks. Since you will be crossing some open water, you should take the weather into account depending on your skill level.

The Y is again a handy place to put-in for this trip, but I'll also mention some other options along the way. Having passed through the Masons Island Causeway, we head east this time away from the island. We are in clamming territory

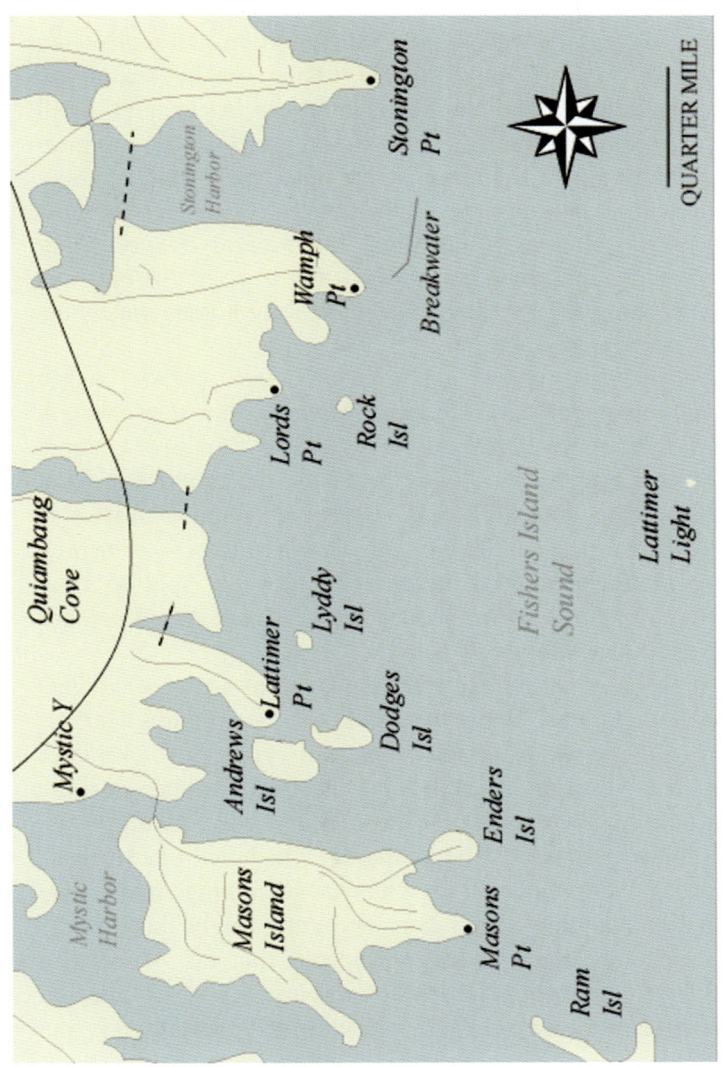

East to Stonington Harbor

QUARTER MILE

here and also beautiful salt marshes and grasses. I tend to head directly for the passage between Andrews Island and Latimer Point although there is a nice body of water on the left that should be worth poking around in. I really like paddling through the channel here. There are houses on the shore, Andrews Island on the right, little docks and small boats. Up until recently, Latimer was a pretty basic, summer-cottage community but, like many other places, it is going upscale with many upgrades to the houses. Some people view this sort of thing as a negative, the natural beauty being spoiled, etc., and they definitely have a point. For me, however, being able to check out interesting homes makes the paddle more interesting.

Andrews Island is a good size and is worth circumnavigating. It and Dodges Island are almost connected. At low tide, there is only a very narrow, shallow channel between the two. This is a great spot to get up close to local wildlife in their natural habitat. Egrets are often seen here as are Canadian geese. There are also a number of osprey nesting platforms around here. It's a lovely spot to float through and take in the rocks and seaweed and smooth stones on the shallow bottom.

Rounding Latimer, you get a great view of Fishers Island Sound, with Wamphassuc Point, Stonington Harbor, Watch Hill, and Napatree Point to your left, Latimer Lighthouse straight ahead and Fishers Island in the background. There is a nice little beach here, at the point, which may be private. The locals have installed one of these floating buoy systems to designate a swimming area. One day, I was steaming across here and cut straight through the buoys since no one was swimming out that far. I heard a shout from the beach, an adult waving his arms angrily. Needless to say, I waved back, wished him a pleasant day, and continued on my way amicably. More than likely, these buoys are illegally blocking water access, so it's a bit much to give a lone kayaker a hard time. There is another little inlet here that I've never explored but looks interesting.

As you head toward Lords Point, you will pass by Quiambaug Cove on the left. There is a very small put-in here near the old Yankee Gas building. You will need to search for it a bit if you want to use it, as it's just through a gap in the wall. It is well worth venturing up the cove, under the railroad bridge and the Route 1 bridge. It is about a mile deep with interesting views all the way until it peters out into a stream. A nice place to go if you want a quiet paddle.

Lords Point has a bigger community than Latimer, and it has also gone upscale. I came out here one Saturday morning in thick fog and really enjoyed it. I tend to kayak much slower and much more cautiously in fog with the result that I take in more of the little that I can see. That's one of life's enigmas, I think. We tend to travel all over the place and see an awful lot of things, but it's only when we get tired and slow down or, indeed, come to a complete stop that we really begin to comprehend what we are looking at. I've had this experience more than once when I have overextended myself, been on the wrong track, or been "forced" to give up goals or ambitions. And out of that small giving up eventually comes a calmness and an acceptance and a realization that all of the small things in life are wondrous, and the big stuff will eventually take care of itself. I think we all experience this, and it is a very unexpected and sometimes unwanted gift of having lived a bit and maturing.

***

So, now that the fog has lifted, we can head on toward Wamphassuc. On our way, we pass tiny Rock Island, which is always covered with egrets and gulls and for this reason best not approached downwind. The Wamphassuc area of Stonington is a very affluent community with many expensive and elegant homes. I believe that there are a couple of

47

compounds here owned by families with names such as Schaeffer (breweries) and Woolworth. Stonington Harbor is around the point and is protected by two long breakwaters, the one on the west close to land and that on the east being farther out. This has got to be one of the most interesting and scenic harbors that I have kayaked with Camden, Maine; Newport, Rhode Island; and Mystic close seconds. In summer, it is peppered with boats, mainly sail, with some motor cruisers. There are many gorgeous, expensive craft moored here. It's a treat to see how our betters live. Needless to say, moorings are at a premium in this harbor, and there is ongoing, internecine feuding between various small-town factions as to how things should be organized and doled out. Thankfully, we, humble yakers, need not bother ourselves with these troublesome matters.

A traditional catboat in Stonington Harbor on a foggy day.

Why not cut straight across the mouth of the harbor to little Dubois Beach so that we can experience the best of

Stonington without delay? Dubois, the town beach on Stonington Point, is a very popular spot for locals and visitors alike. There is a good-size parking area where lots of people sit and watch the boating world go by. The beach provides good harbor access for kayaks but not during swimming hours when lifeguards are on duty. I learned to scuba a number of years back, and I practiced my skills here at Dubois once or twice with a friend. It did not work out too well. I was a novice (still am!), and a thick wetsuit, heavy weights, low visibility, and a lot of eelgrass did not make for a great experience. Plus, I dropped my weight belt in the eelgrass and had a lot of trouble finding it. Having said all of this, I am still interested in exploring the bottom here. Local lore has it that the hurricane of '38 blew an enormous amount of household effects (and houses!) into the water, so much so that this patch of water was called "the kitchen sink."

As you head into the harbor, you will see an old mill on your right. I suppose that this was a bustling factory back when industry and industrial labor were not unfashionable around here. This was built originally to make machinery for velvet mills, then it was converted into a molding facility for plastic components. These days, the notion of an actual factory with workers in it would not be tolerated in this museum-quality town. The mill has now been transformed into luxury condominiums facing and abutting the water. Part of the permitting for this project included a very nice public walkway along the water. Just by the walkway are new, private slips where some gorgeous boats are docked.

This immediate locality has had an extraordinary recent history of devastating fires. The first, about six years ago, destroyed the beautiful, beloved Harbor-View restaurant. This was truly a gem with a very comfortable bar and restaurant and a rich, warm atmosphere. A very nice B&B inn has now been built on the site, which is a bit of comfort. A second, much bigger, conflagration recently gutted the old mill factory even as it was being converted to apartments. This

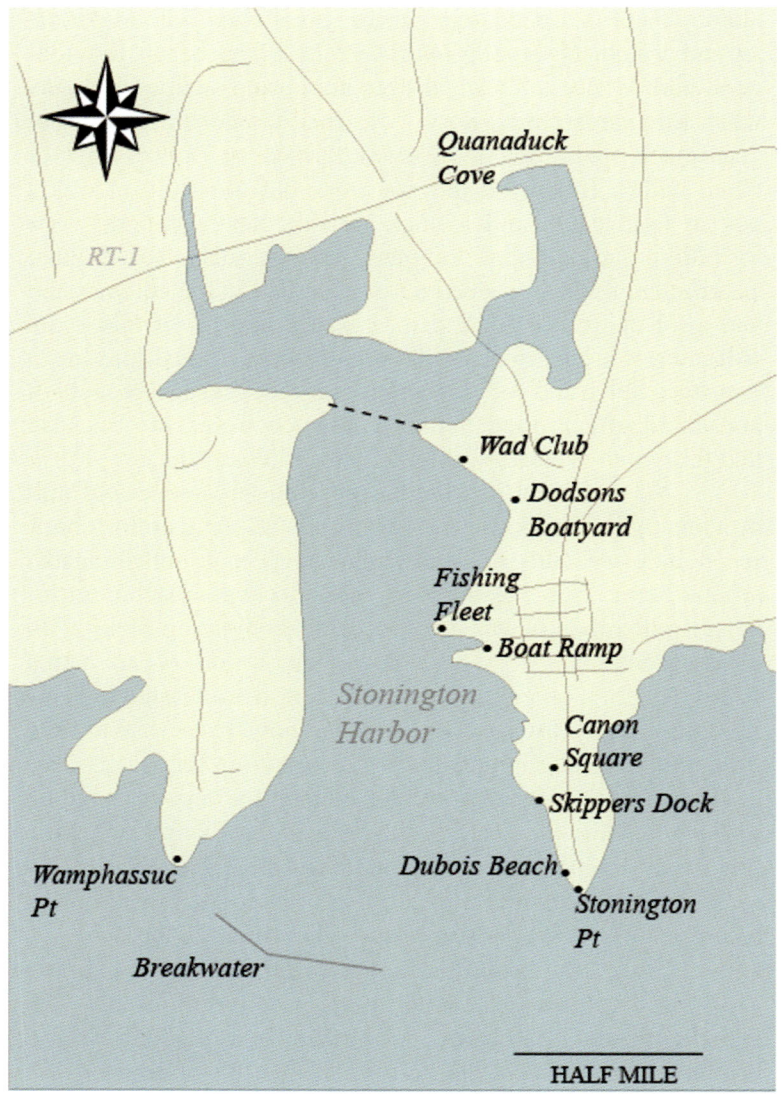

Stonington Harbor

fire was so fierce that it severely scorched multiple, wooden homes across the little street. Having seen the evidence of the scorching, I can only say that the inhabitants of the houses were very, very lucky. Beyond the mill, you pass Skippers restaurant with its long extended dock where boaters can pick up take-away meals. Farther on, you come upon the fishing fleet at the town pier. This is one of the most vibrant, living remnants of Stonington's heritage.

Sometime in the nineteenth century, Stonington was visited by migrant fishing boats from the Azores. Quite a paddle! Portuguese fishermen subsequently settled here, and this was the genesis of the Stonington fleet. There are still many Portuguese families and names in the town and also, the curiously designated, Portuguese Holy Ghost Society, which, of course, is centered 'round a bar but is located in a formidable granite building. Every year the bishop of Norwich blesses the fleet in a colorful procession of boats from the town dock out to the breakwaters. There is a festival and parade associated with the event, but the need for the blessings is very real as the loss of fishermen at sea is not a rare occurrence, unfortunately, in this community.

Near the fleet, in a little key, is the "small boat association" put-in ramp. This is an excellent place to beach or set out from. Take an hour or two to explore the borough from here. Water Street is two hundreds yards away and is resplendent with galleries, antique shops, stores, and a few restaurants. There is a nice little deli on this street called Noni's, and the owners' great uncle was the Crean who accompanied Shakleton to the South Pole. Make no mistake about it; Stonington is a picture-perfect coastal village, more so than Mystic, which, while also pretty, is very much a working town. To the borough's credit, they have several nice wooden benches outside the shops that make for a good place to take a rest in the sun or shade. As you stroll up toward the point, you will come to the small town square, which has a cannon and cannonballs from the War of 1812. This whole area is very rich in stories of the war. At one point, the British navy blockaded Stonington from the sea. The local militia were roused and they were ready and anxious to defend the town. The story is told of the Brits launching a long boat with a crew of marines, aiming to land on the east of Stonington Point only to have the boat sunk and a marine killed by a very lucky cannon shot from the shore. The Brits never made it ashore, and a stanza from the American national anthem is reputed to have been based on this little battle. Heading in the opposite direction on Water Street, you will come to the town green, the library, and the Catholic church. If you want to see the Holy Ghost Society, head one street over from Noni's to Main Street, which has many fine buildings in a classic Greek style.

***

The cozy bar at Boom restaurant in Stonington Harbor.

You've had your rest and refreshments, so let's head back to the water. Going deeper into the harbor, beyond the trawlers, are some very attractive waterside homes. Stonington has house and garden tours at least once during the summer. I've never gone, but I'm sure it's worth trying if only to see their water views. Toward the back of the harbor is Dodsons Boatyard, which is a bit of an institution around here. It runs a water taxi to the sailboats and has a lovely restaurant called Boom and an interesting little marina store in its yard. The docks here are also a great place to see some very beautiful and expensive boats. As you swing west at the back of the harbor, you pass the Wadawadnack club, known locally as the Wad. This is a private tennis and yacht club with a great view of the harbor. Off season (<u>well</u> off season), there is no one to stop you from beaching here and sitting on the seawall or lawn to picnic, rest, or just gaze at the scenery.

Nearby is the ubiquitous Amtrak railway line with another series of beautiful coves accessed under the railway-bridge and causeways. These coves have names I can hardly pronounce like "Quanaduck" and "Wikkaty." You can't fail to notice in this part of the world that a lot of places have long, strange (to the European ear), rhythmic Native American names. Quanaduck cove is very pretty, and you can paddle up under the railway bridge as far as the well-maintained condominiums that abut Route 1. On the far side of the harbor, on Wamphassuc, a series of huge, spectacular homes have recently been built with the not unexpected controversy as to whether this is a good or a bad thing. From my perspective, the homes are far away enough from the borough not to be much of an impact. Also, I know a couple of people living there, so I'd better keep quiet!

***

Other than the sleek boats, there is not a lot of anything special as you paddle back to the mouth of the harbor. This time, we will make a beeline back to Ram Island on our return journey. Or if you feel more comfortable, you can keep a little closer to the shore by touching on Dodges, then Enders, and finally Ram Islands. This is a good pull across here. If you are warmed up, in a good place, and accompanied by one or two good friends, it's a great leg to get a strong, brisk stroke going and tell a couple of stories as you go.

John and I had an exciting experience in this area a couple of years ago. It was in the summer, and we had rendezvoused near the Y around five thirty in the evening to paddle to Stonington. The day was heavy and humid with thunderstorms forecast, but we ventured out regardless. You probably know what it's like; we had not been out for a while; work was grinding and oppressive, and we had set our sights earlier in the day on some relief. This is often a dangerous mood as you end up desperate to stick with plan A regardless of the consequences. Anyway, we headed down the river and then east. I think we got as far as Wamphassuc when we could no longer ignore the warning signs.

> *The wind had bundled up the clouds, high over Knocknarae,*
>
> *And thrown the thunder on the stones for all that Maeve could say.*

We decided to head back and faced into the long paddle to Latimer Point. Although the storm was not yet upon us, the sky was half-filled with heavy gray clouds topped with thunderheads. The distant rumbles began to be replaced with nearby, sudden sharp cracks and associated illuminations. We briefly considered trying to make it all the way home, but thankfully, fear won out; and we pulled in abruptly at Latimer Point boat ramp. At this time, the heavens opened, so we dragged the boats ashore and ran for whatever cover we could find. The best we could do was crouch in under a long boat rack, protected a little from the rain by upturned wooden dinghies. We sat out the storm there, sitting on our butts like hobos, chatting all the while. We had a dilemma, of course. Here we were, sitting on our haunches in the middle of a violent storm, our loved ones at home fearing the worst and no obvious way of making it back. John had a cell phone! We called Karen, and she came with my old station wagon to pick us up. She was none too happy with this tomfoolery either, and let us know it too. We still joke about this, if we are miles away from home, "maybe we should call Karen?"

Wouldn't you know it? We've been talking so much that we are at Dodges and Enders already! It always feels more exposed as you head out around the seawall here at Enders. It's a mixture of fact and mind-set. There is a lot of open water to your left, and the seawall on your right separates the boater from the comfort of the familiar features of the island; and you feel more alone because of this.

Ram Island is about half a mile long, give or take, and sits just beyond the mouth of the Mystic River. It is L-shaped with the concave aspect facing approximately east. There is at least one home on it, and the owners steam to and from the "mainland" in a tough-looking motor cruiser with a rusty exhaust pipe protruding from the cabin roof. It's a very nice and interesting island to explore from the water in good weather. In stormy weather, it is cold and unfriendly because of its exposure. I paddled out there one afternoon in late October as I returned from a trip to Quiambaug Cove. I approached the northern tip where there are a couple of rocky promontories, which are normally connected together but separated at low tide. That evening the water was still; the sun was setting over Morgan Point, and the milieu was magical. The tide was ebbing, and this exposed a shallow sandbar between the island and the rocks. I floated up to the bar and rested there to experience the beauty and stillness. At higher tides, it's fun to glide through here, especially when the water is moving fast. Farther south, the island forms a pretty little cove that is quite sheltered and has a nice sandy beach. You often see boats anchored here just to rest and take in the views, I would imagine.

Well, we've been out for quite a while now, and it's more than time to make our way back to the Y and home to some comfort; so I will bid you adieu for the moment. If you are a little tired from your exertions, you will probably want to make your way back by heading directly upriver rather than taking the longer route around Masons Island.

5

Tuesday Night Paddlers

(Loose association. Growing flotilla. Spectacular accident on Poquonnock River. Paddlers' schedule.)

The Tuesday Night Paddlers, a.k.a., the "Paddlers," are a great local kayaking group that John, Stuart, myself, and other friends belong to. It's a unique association, in that you don't really belong to anything; you just turn up! It was started in 1997 by a couple of friends, Marty, Bill and others, as a way of getting together regularly on the water. There is no membership although there are a few, sensible rules if you want to kayak with the group; safety, responsibility, and the like. A schedule is published by a few core members, and in the first couple of years, this was mainly limited to Tuesday evening events from April to September. The hunting grounds for the paddlers now extend anywhere from the Thimble Islands to Newport, although most of the trips range from New London County to Charleston, Rhode Island. The Tuesday night events begin at 5:30 to 6 PM depending on the time of year. They typically cover six to ten miles of interesting coastline and you are on the water for about three hours. The schedule and list of locations is available within the group by mailing list, and each week's paddle is usually posted in local newspapers, especially the Mystic broadsheets.

The Tuesday Night Paddler group preparing to embark from the small Boat association beach in Stonington Harbor.

I became aware of the Paddlers the same year that I bought my first kayak. It was probably through John as we were working together in a management team at the time. We joined them for the first event of the year at Esker Point in April. I had great expectations for the night; to head out into uncharted waters for a couple of hours of adventure with interesting companions. There were about ten boats in the water when I arrived, and the wind was blowing a bit. To my disappointment, the leaders of the group decided that it was too blustery to head out into the Sound so early in the year, given that the water temperature was still barely fifty degrees. We headed under the Groton Long Point causeway and the railway bridge instead (yes, more of these!) and up into Palmers Cove. While this is a pleasant cove, it is no more than half a mile deep. In addition, the air and water temperature and the grayness of the skies made it a pretty dreary paddle. My abiding memory of the evening is of mild disappointment. They were a nice, ordinary bunch of souls though. Little did I know that this was the beginning of a rich association for me, and many interesting adventures.In those days, the Paddlers were a small group, typically no more than five to fifteen people on a trip. I found it very intimate and sociable with the small numbers and got to know Bill, Marty, Stan and others well through chats on and off the water. We were also well organized, waiting a reasonable time for everyone to put in and declaring a route and destination before we set out. Also, we counted the number of boats in our fleet at the beginning of each trip and had a "no kayaker left behind" policy once we got going. My impressions of this being a risk-averse group quickly evaporated as I got to know everyone and was left trailing routinely.

These are strong kayakers! I cannot keep up with many of them if they paddle hard for a sustained period of time. Also, I'm a little lazy, and sadly my muscles and joints are not what they were. It's an old story, which I'll gladly tell you if you buy me a beer and pay attention. Besides the camaraderie, the great thing about the group is that it gets you out and about the coastline to see different areas every week.

Each Tuesday night, there are different starting points. Anywhere within a five-mile radius, you will see fellow paddlers converging on the designated put-in with boats perched on their cars, wagons, and trucks. There is the ritual of unloading, gearing up, and launching, and we all help each other with this. Someone is always late, so we wait for them as long as makes sense before heading off to Stonington, Waterford beach, Niantic, Watch Hill, Quiambaug Cove, or whatever that night's destination is. It's always fun, and we have had many memorable evenings. Once a month or so, we will have a full-moon paddle.

Most, if not all, of the trips that are described in this book are encompassed by a full-year Paddlers schedule. If you visit this area during spring, summer, or fall, I would strongly recommend hooking up with them for an evening.

Over the years, the group has evolved and changed. Just recently, I asked Bill and Marty for back issues of the schedules. Marty graciously obliged, and her archive of annual schedules told the history of the group. Formed in June 1997 with a handwritten invitation to paddle at Esker Point. There was a thirteen-night schedule in '98 ranging from the Thames River to Barn Island. The following year there were seventeen trips, when John and I joined. By 2002, we had a website, twenty-seven events, many at the weekends, and a wide range of destinations.

Before the advent of the website, the group was small and quite disciplined. We knew our route, stayed together, and waited for stragglers. You were always paddling with familiar faces. The group ballooned once the schedule hit the web. It was not unusual, on a good night, to have a flotilla of up to forty boats paddling the sounds. It was quite a sight, and I imagine that many a sailor looked twice to check us out. With size came complexity and little cliques. The professionals would race off at a ferocious pace leaving everyone else behind. Then came the average paddlers and lastly stragglers and latecomers. Destinations became more malleable. We often came down the Mystic River trailing the larger group to see the pros heading for Fishers Island, the average paddlers heading for Stonington Harbor, and stragglers confused as to what they should do. I was pleasantly impressed, two years ago, to learn that our founding members were considering means of curtailing this exuberance of growth. The group has since shrunk back to a more comfortable size. Having said that, the number of excursions is now over four dozen ranging from the Thimble Islands to Middletown Connecticut, to Fort Wetherill Rhode Island.

We have had many wonderful nights with the paddlers. One I remember in particular was from the Peruzotti

(Groton Town) boat launch to Mumford Cove. The departure point, near the Groton-New London Airport and the railroad bridge, is from an unimpressive, small slimy ramp. It's a long pull down the Poquonnock River before you reach Bushy Point to enter the sound. I always assumed that the magnitude of this paddle was more psychological than real given that the whole point is to get out to the sound and explore. However, on checking my charts, I find that it is indeed a two-mile pull approximately. A spectacular accident occurred here on the

Thimble Islands in late October.

river a couple of years back. A corporate Lear Jet was coming in to land, and sadly one of the pilots apparently made an error with the flaps, diving the plane into rooftops and crashing spectacularly into the river. Both pilots were killed, but local residents whose houses were hit managed to escape injury by diving out through windows and the like. Can you just imagine what it would have been like to be yaking on the river when all that happened? Sine then there have been *two* other, similar crashes in the waters near the airport!

When we rounded Bushy Point on the evening, I'm describing, we were faced with a strong headwind and four-foot seas from the beam. We had a very exciting paddle to reach the beach at Bluff Point, and it was a miracle that no one went in. This was one of the times when you were almost out of control, the advanced paddlers bracing expertly and the rest of us paddling frantically and half bracing to keep moving and stay upright. The waves were coming at us from behind as we turned toward the beach, and we were surfing forward with alarmingly little control over direction, fearful of being turned abeam and overturned. Some of us beached nearby to rest and take stock. Eventually, we followed the rest of the pack around Bluff Point and into sheltered Mumford Cove. We rested there on the back side of Groton Long Point, outside the Venetian harbor, and listened to Marty regale us on the mating habits of horseshoe crabs, which were scattered in abundance along the beach. We had our little picnic, an apple, snack, and soda, and then began to head back. The wind and tide had changed by then, and we had an easy return journey but still a long pull up the river.

A compilation of put in locations and directions from a recent Paddlers schedule is at the end of this book. I can't think of a better guide to kayaking in this part of the world. It describes how to get to all of the best put-in's and also provides excellent suggestions with regard to destinations.

6

Groton Long Point and Beyond

(Mouse Island. Battle of Fort Hill. Skip hatched a plan. Lazarus arose. Summer concerts.)

So far, all of our trips have started from the Mystic River. This is also true of heading west toward Groton Long Point and the Thames River. Every year, I count with my fingers the interesting paddles that can be taken from Mystic, and I always end up using both hands and occasionally a foot or two. We will begin this trip from Morgan Point at the mouth of the river. Right at the point, you will see little Mouse Island, which is home to a couple of flimsy cottages. There are a number of big rocks as you turn west, and you can slip through here at most tides.

John and I were paddling near here one August, heading toward Esker Point about an hour before dusk. On our way back, as the sun was setting, we slipped through the "middle" of Mouse Island, this section being almost submerged at high tide. We were enchanted to see that the southern end of this tiny island was softly illuminated with dozens of candles placed there by summer residents. The lights were scattered around, some near the house and more right down by the water. A whole family was outside with one or two adults catching bluefish from the rocks. It is hard to do full justice to this lovely scene as we lingered near the island, drinking in the panoply of lights and their reflections on the still water, with noisy shoals of bluefish breaking nearby. This experience illustrates the obvious point, that if you do not get out on the water you will not be present when magical moments like this occur!

***

Right beside the lighthouse is another weathered, shingled home with a dock that extends about fifty feet out into the water. This is the home of a former chief of the Mashantucket Pequot Indians; we'll call him Skip. The chief is a character by any measure. He is the visionary who led his people in gaining recognition as a legitimate Indian tribe with sovereign rights over their reservation lands. It's hard to know where to start with this; it's such a rich story. Much of it is well-known and publicized, not all of this positive or balanced. The simple facts are that the tribe was settled in Ledyard, Connecticut, after the battle of Fort Hill in 1637. They led a poor, subsistence life there for many a long year. Some intermarried with African Americans, a fact that is thrown in their faces in recent years as a reason for shame. This to me is a double whammy; you are viewed as inferior as you are and then doubly so for partnering with someone from another wronged race.

In the 1970s, the tribe, like many a Catholic church, built a bingo hall and thrived modestly. Building on this success, Skip hatched a plan to gain federal recognition of the tribe as a sovereign entity, the prize being that revenue on their own lands would be free of all federal and state taxes. Now there's an idea whose time might come! The big goal

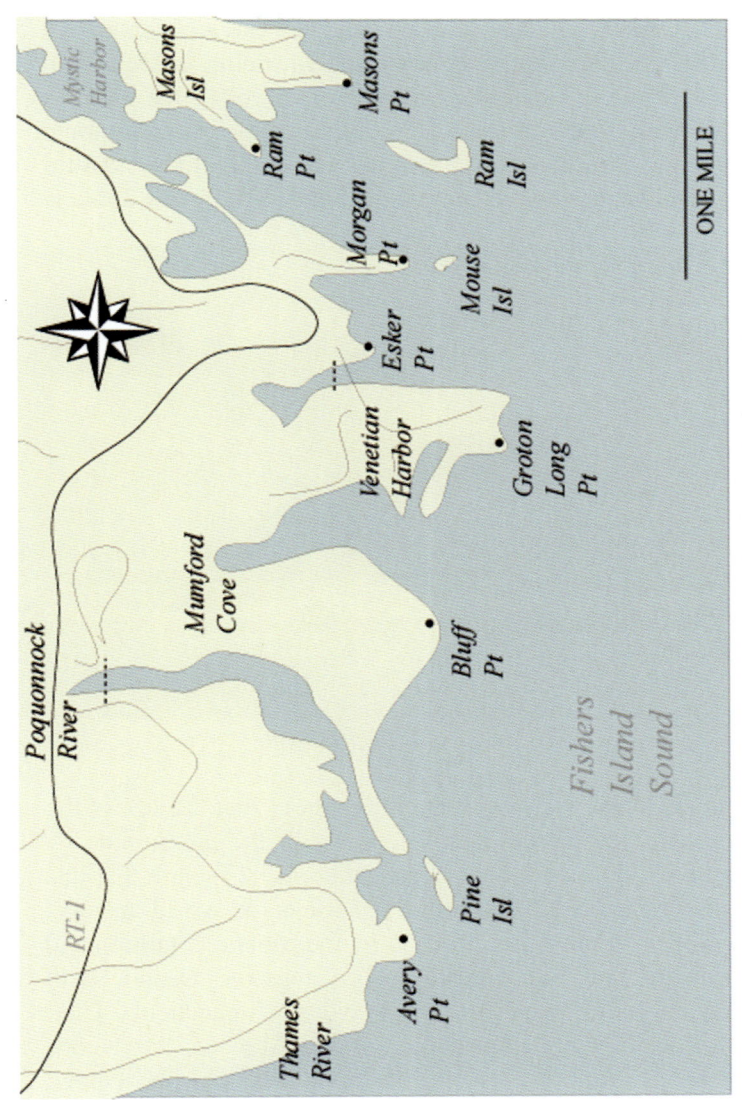

Masons Isl

Mystic Harbor

Masons Pt

Ram Pt

Ram Isl

Morgan Pt

Mouse Isl

Esker Pt

Venetian Harbor

Groton Long Pt

Mumford Cove

Poquonnock River

Bluff Pt

Fishers Island Sound

RT-1

Pine Isl

Avery Pt

Thames River

ONE MILE

Groton Long Point and Beyond

was an Indian casino in the heart of the northeast. Skip had some significant advocates and adversaries in this endeavor. By all accounts, the big banks would not advance capital to the tribe. In the absence of domestic financing, a Malaysian family with major gambling interests bankrolled the Pequots handsomely, no doubt for a rich return. Some of the region's Democratic politicians, Dodd in particular, gave skillful assistance in steering the Bureau of Indian Affairs bill through

Morgan Point Lighthouse.

Congress. There is a very contentious story that the size of the reservation was increased considerably at the last minute by some fancy map work behind closed doors. I'm sure that this has never happened before in American or world history! Many local people were incensed by the tribal recognition and the construction and opening of a massive casino, with subsequent major expansions, in Ledyard, Connecticut. Their reaction is very understandable. The advent of "Foxwoods Casino" has changed the pace and feel of what used be a quiet, rural New England town. To add insult to injury, a second tribe, the Mohegans, opened a similar-size casino nearby following federal recognition of their reservation a few years later. The advent of these mammoth casinos has been widely reported upon in local and national media.

There are several accounts of Skip's and the tribe's recent history, not all of them flattering. They have many of the challenges of the newly rich, exacerbated by inadequate education and a paucity of good role models. You have to empathize with local residents who have worked hard, paying their taxes to create a decent life only to see Native Americans leapfrog to preeminence on the back of an industry that has a definite dark side. All of these views and feelings are played out in local newspapers and books. But another perspective is of an Indian tribe, displaced and marginalized, and, in Ledyard, Connecticut, the greatest comeback since Lazarus by the Mashantucket Pequots. A great yarn by any standards!

***

As you head north, away from Morgan Point and into West Cove, you will pass a variety of new waterside homes on your right. There is a marina at the back of the cove, I think it may be Spicer's, but I've never found it that interesting, at least from the water. A little farther west is Esker Point, which is the Groton Town beach, and quite busy in the summer season. There are volleyball courts on the sand, a food concession, bathrooms, and showers, and it is open to everyone! The town organizes rock and blues concerts on the beach here in the summer months. These are well worth attending, either from the land or the water. Hundreds of local residents turn out to picnic, socialize, and enjoy the music. It's American small-town culture at its best. Across the road from the beach is the Fishermans Restaurant, which is very well liked for its casual, comfortable atmosphere and food.

There is a headland beyond the beach and beyond that Palmer Cove and Groton Long Point. The whole sweep that runs from Morgan Point to Groton Long Point is very pretty and somewhat protected. Long Point is a private community association within, but separate from, the town of Groton. It has its own small police force and zoning rules. It is very appealing with beautiful homes, interesting lagoons and wetlands, and two glorious beaches. One of these reminds me of French Atlantic beaches, crescent in shape with a small boardwalk and traditional coastal cottages a few feet back from the strand. It's stunning in high summer. Just beyond,

A 44 foot J-boat near the lighthouse at the mouth of the Thames River in New London.

and well hidden, is the entrance to a stylish, Venetian harbor that runs east, behind and parallel to the beach. Its banks are crowded with beautiful homes as one might see in the Florida Keys and the owners boats are moored and docked within easy reach. As you paddle farther west, Long Point leads to Mumford Cove and then Bluff Point. The cove is a lovely, natural inlet with pristine marshlands to explore. Bluff Point is a nature preserve with hiking trails and a great natural asset to the local community. The beach on the ocean side of Bluff Point is accessed either by a longish hike from the parking lot, near the airport or by boat. It is a long, sweeping unspoiled stretch of sand and rarely crowded because of its remoteness. This is a beautiful stretch of natural coastline to explore.

7

An Industrious River

(University architecture. Drugs and Subs. Hilary Clinton hits the bottle. Blood on the Thames.)

Bayberry Lane is a good place to begin an exploration of Avery Point, the Thames River, and the Waterford shoreline. The public boat launch here is a good put in, and you are soon out among the mooring fields near Shennecosset Yacht Club. You head west toward Avery Point, which is home to a college of the University of Connecticut and also Project Oceanology, a marine environmental research center. Project O' conducts tours of the waters around here including hands-on research activities, which is a great experience for kids and adults alike. The university buildings at Avery Point are a curious collection of architectural styles including the large Tudor-style mansion that was built in 1903. There is also a new marine-sciences laboratory building, which is a large barn-like structure. I'm tempted to say that this building is from the "f*** you" school of architecture to quote Bill Bryson, but realistically, the Thames River is very much an industrial

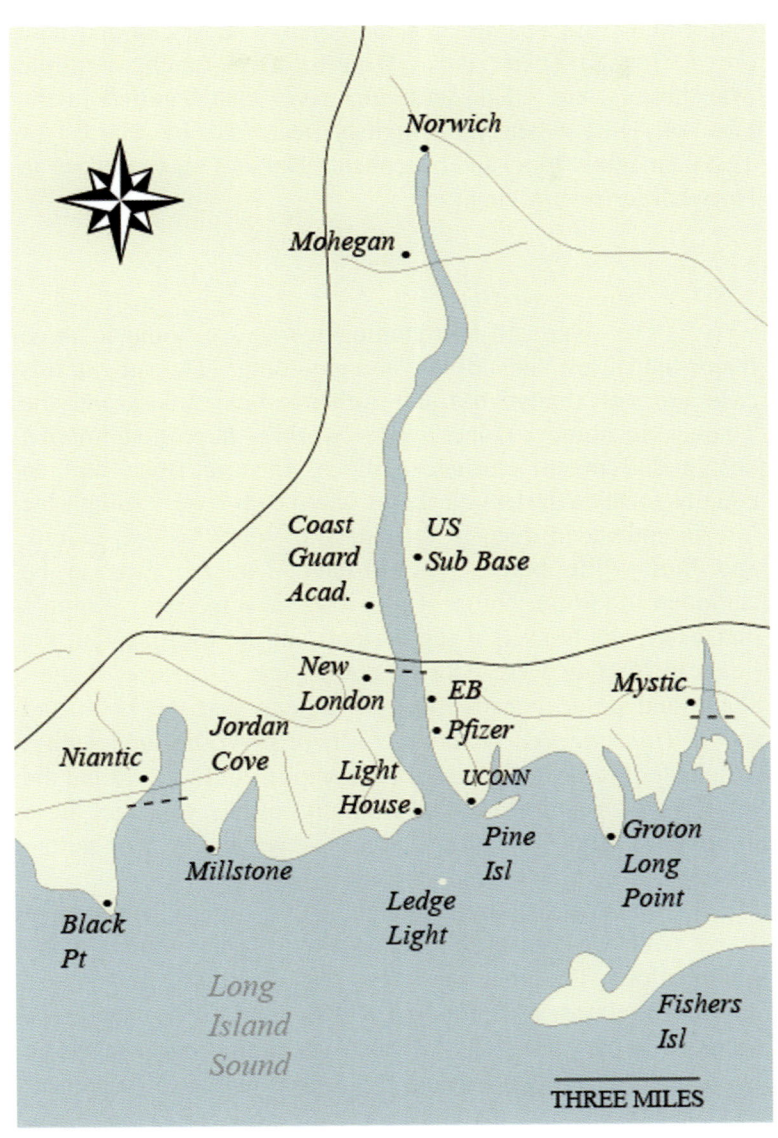

The Thames River

center; so there is really no point in picking on UConn. Speaking of the Thames, the old-country names around here are a riot!   There is a Waterford, Norwich, multiple Manchesters, etc.   This particular river also featured in the War of 1812 when the English fleet, led by Hardy, of Trafalgar fame, blockaded Stephen Decatur's ships upriver at Norwich for several months.

***

The river and surrounding towns are home to three major industries: subs, drugs, and gambling! The subs in this case are not sandwiches but rather submersibles, and the Thames is home to one of the world's largest submarine design and manufacturing facilities, Electric Boat, and an equally formidable United States Navy, sub-base. Submarine lore is embedded deep in the fabric of local history, culture and family life here.   The ill-fated *Thresher* was to be stationed in Groton before it met it's gruesome fate. Karen's dad, Hal, was himself a submariner, and he told me that the boats in his day were called "sewer pipes" because of their shape and crude construction. I believe that the book and movie *Hunt for Red October* is set, in parts, in our locality. Whenever the United States is involved in conflicts around the world, which unfortunately is pretty often, you see these mammoth, black craft glide down the river and hear of sailors leaving home for extended periods.

I was present at the launching of a sub at Electric Boat about twelve years back, and it was a great treat for the imagination. The boat was a Los Angeles class, and it was enormous, almost four hundred feet long and weighing seven thousand tons. This was the last American submarine to be launched on "wooden ways." It was fascinating to be present and witness the juxtaposition of the most modern, sophisticated engineering and electronics with the wood and carpentry-based processes with which the Venetians launched their sailboats in the Middle Ages. The submarine itself is built in a hanger (over several years) which slopes down to the water.

As the day and hour of the launch approach, armies of carpenters craft a huge, V-shaped wooden cradle the length of the hull and then drive in wedges to raise the cradle so that it begins to take the weight of the boat. Once this process has been started, the boat begins to move, imperceptibly at first, but once begun, the launch must then take place within a finite period of time; or else the sub will launch itself. At the same time as the wedges are being driven in, another small army applies tons of grease to the wooden ways to help speed the boat on its way.

At the appointed hour, the dignitary who will "launch" the boat, in this case Hillary Clinton, makes a very short speech and bursts a bottle of champagne off the hull. At the same time, the last remaining restraints on the boat are removed. The submarine begins to move, slowly at first, but rapidly gains speed as it thunders down the "wooden ways." It slices into the water with a huge splash and bounces back up to the delighted roar of the crowd. Overall, a sight to be seen, to be believed!

The "drugs" connection on the river is the Pfizer Pharmaceuticals R&D and manufacturing campus, which sit right beside Electric Boat, downstream of the interstate bridge. Having explained subs and drugs on the Thames River, the gambling associations, of course, are the Mashantucket and Mohegan casinos. At one time the Mashantuckets operated a high-speed ferry, which was berthed in New London. This boat on various occasions plied the waters to New York, Martha's Vineyard, and other nearby destinations. It was the brainchild of the aforementioned Skip, and he also envisioned a ferry-construction facility locally, which sadly never came to pass. The Mohegan Casino can be seen from the river near Norwich, and they have a fireworks display every Wednesday in the summer months. I must confess that I have not kayaked

Ledge Light, photographed from the rocks at Eastern Point beach.

that much on the Thames. I did learn to sail here however in a dingy club. I am an average sailor at best. It generally takes me quite a while to gain proficiency in activities that require a high degree of coordination, where the right hand is doing one thing while the left hand is doing something totally different. I remember one infamous afternoon, racing with colleagues near the New London shore. I was at the helm, and my "crew" was a mild-mannered pharmacist who I am sure wanted nothing other than a pleasant couple of hours on the water. The time came to tack, and I swung the tiller around suddenly, with no warning to my partner, with the result that he was hit sharply in the temple by the swinging boom. A small amount of blood began to flow, but I apologized profusely; and we continued on. At the next mark, a jibe was called for, which I executed badly again, and my hapless crew was cracked on the other temple with the boom.

By that time, however, we were both in trouble. The wind had picked up considerably, and with our sails in disarray, the boat was overpowered; and we were both plunged into the water. To add insult to injury, my colleague's wallet slipped out of his pocket as he fell in and went floating away with the tide. To his everlasting credit, he neither hit me nor cursed me nor, to my knowledge at least, bad-mouthed me after we had limped back to shore. After this awful experience, I decided to further my sailing skills by going out alone to learn in light winds, and this worked out well as you can take your time with all maneuvers without worrying about any dire impact on others.

Friends and I have crossed the mouth of the Thames a number of times. It's about two miles across from Pine Island to Ocean Beach. You do have to watch out for boat traffic, particularly ferries. If the high-speed variety happens along, it's fun to paddle across the wake, not at all as dangerous as you would think (if you know what you are doing, of course). New London is a regular host to tall-ships gatherings, and John has experienced the huge parade of boats in his kayak and raves about it. There is also the possibility to be on the water at the right time as a large submarine passes by on the surface, which must be an awesome experience. On the occasions when we have crossed over, we tend to head for Waterford Town Beach and land there to picnic and swim. If you go farther, there is some beautiful paddling near Harkness Park and Seaside with golden beaches and historic homes. Well worth the trip!

8

East of Stonington

(Sandy Point. The Long Island Express. Watch Hill. Winnepaug in autumn.)

Since I came to live in the Mystic area, I have developed an abiding prejudice that east rather than west is the best direction to wander. This was established early on through train and car rides to New York City and the strong sense that natural beauty ebbs a bit once you go south of New Haven. This bias has carried over into my kayaking rambles, and I tend to feel most at home when I turn east out of the Mystic River. So you will understand why I am equally fond of heading east from Stonington Harbor to Watch Hill and beyond. You can begin these paddles from the "small boat association" ramp in Stonington Harbor or from Dubois Beach.

Last Labor Day weekend, Karen and I decided to kayak from Stonington to Sandy Point to picnic and swim. The day was pretty blustery with winds of fifteen to twenty knots. There had been a boating accident nearby the day before. Three or four friends were out fishing together, in even higher winds, in a small boat on the Watch Hill reefs. A succession of waves swamped their boat, and they all went in the water. Although help arrived pretty quickly, one of their number had already died, perhaps from a heart attack. That's the way it is on the water. You have to be so careful, and at the same time, you are out there to be carefree.

We intended to launch from Dubois Beach, but the lifeguard turned us away as the beach was reserved for sunbathers and swimmers but also advised us not to go out because of the wind. I think that she was naturally, somewhat over-sensitized by the previous day's tragedy, as the water at the point was choppy but very manageable. Someone steered us toward a put-in on the east side of the borough, which turned out to be a tiny beach down a little dead-end street. We set out from there, paddling down a short canal, past a swimmer resting on a floating dock and a beautiful wooden, cabin cruiser. On the left here is a partial island called Salt Acres. This island hosted a Stonington zoning frenzy in recent years, tormenting a corporate executive who sought successive building permits for, first a fifteen-thousand-square-foot home then thirteen and ten until he gave up in the end.

The paddle across to Sandy Point can be challenging due to currents and heavy boat traffic. We stayed out of the channel until we reached the buoy at the northern tip of the point and waited for a gap in the flow of boats to dart across. We were aided by a Stonington water-patrol officer who waved us across at an opportune time.

Karen is a good novice kayaker. The first time we paddled together, we started at the north end of Masons Island and paddled east to south around the island heading toward Enders. I must admit that I was a little bit sneaky in bringing her farther than she actually volunteered for. When she suggested that we go back, I slyly pointed out that it was equidistant to retrace our steps or continue with the circumnavigation. She seemed a little more contemplative

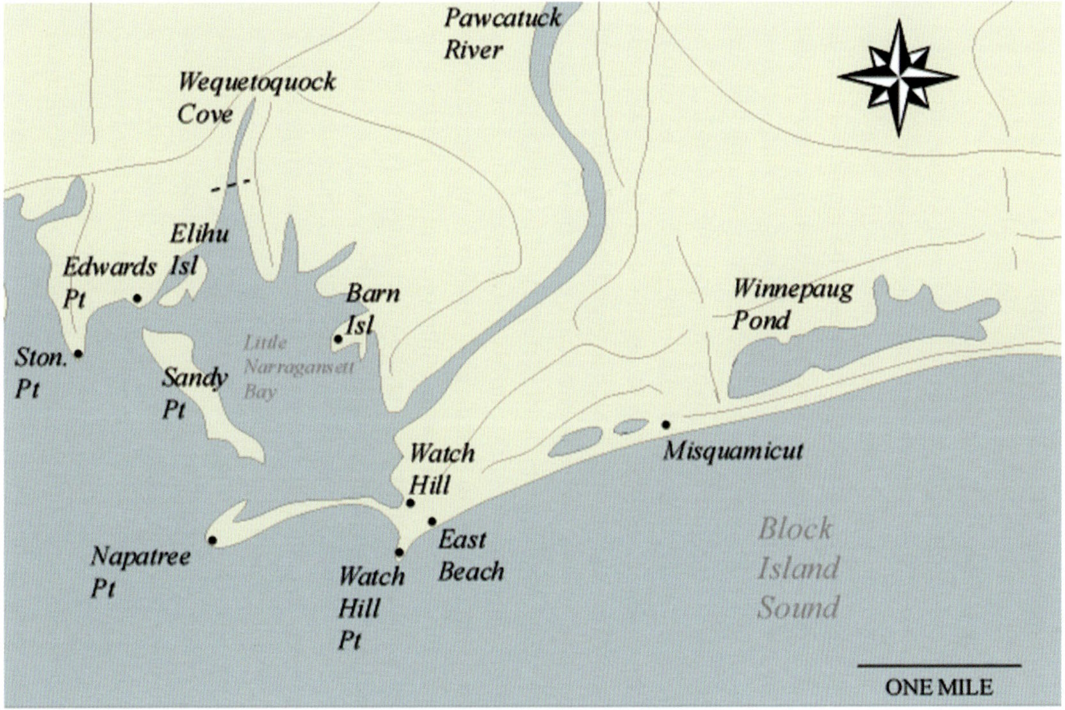

Watch Hill, Rhode Island

Pawcatuck River

Winnepaug Pond

Misquamicut

Block Island Sound

ONE MILE

Wequetoquock Cove

Elihu Isl

Edwards Pt

Ston. Pt

Sandy Pt

Barn Isl

Little Narragansett Bay

Napatree Pt

Watch Hill

East Beach

Watch Hill Pt

79

after this as if she now had a deeper understanding of what the Buddha meant about life being difficult. Thankfully, we made it home without too much hardship, just some blisters on Karen's hands. One thing that impresses me about her kayaking is that when the chips are down she is tough. So when we needed to dart, she darted.

Sandy Point is another popular jewel in our area. It's a mile-long spit of grassy dunes that's accessible only by boat but can get quite crowded. The eastern side is a favorite sunbathing spot for many local families who motor out here in high summer and pass the day lazily swimming, resting and chatting with friends. It's a favorite haunt of Ann, a close friend of Karen's, and they found each other quickly that Sunday as I continued to kayak around the sandbar. The paddle was pretty uneventful although you had to be careful with the breakers off the beach on the west side. With the paddling over, we sat with Karen's friend and her husband and two boys swapping stories as the boats went by.

The boating scene here is mighty. It's hard to believe it, but the only way to get from Mystic, Stonington and all of Fishers Island Sound to Watch Hill Harbor is via the channel between Edwards Point (near Stonington) and the northern tip of Sandy Point. A quick look at the charts suggests that this is the last place you would want to go, and that's why, one day, I spent three hours in my four-foot draft sailboat, trying to travel from Watch Hill to Stonington via the south end of Sandy Point. There is a great expanse of water here, but most of it is only two to three feet deep at low tides. Having grounded here in shallow water for the umpteenth time, I did the unthinkable and asked for directions. Those directions I received were so incredible to me (north around Sandy Point) that I had to ground another couple of times before I relented and followed them. And yes, in case you happened to be there that day, I had to be towed off of one of the groundings.

Mystic, Stonington, Watch Hill, and Fishers Island are all very popular boating destinations in summer, and all of that marine traffic has to funnel through the narrow channel at the tip of Sandy Point. This made for an interesting vista that Labor Day Sunday, a colorful parade of boats just twenty feet from where we were sitting having our picnic. Hundreds of craft, fifty-foot sailboats, cabin cruisers, sports-fishing boats, dinghies, and the like. And a little heightened anxiety as well. "Don't go too fast or stay too close. Watch out for the harbor patrol." Fortunately, or not, there were no significant mishaps although the potential for one kept us entertained. At the end of this great afternoon, Karen and I paddled off into the sunset as our friends boarded their powerboat. We must have made a very pretty and romantic couple as we headed off toward the borough. I would not have changed places with Ann and her crew for anything, although we were wet and a bit sandy and slimy and also faced a lot of schlepping of gear before we even got to our car. Well, not unless they had offered!

***

Northeast of Sandy Point is an area that I have not explored extensively. There is Elihu Island and Wequetequock Cove and Barn Island, which is not a real island. Barn Island is a nature preserve, and one of the Tuesday-night paddles begins at Walkers Dock there. Nor have I explored the Pawcatuck River although it's a good couple of miles of inland waterway. The reason for these omissions is simple gluttony. You come out of beautiful Stonington Harbor. You are looking at Salt Acres, Sandy Point, Fishers Island, Napatree Point, and Watch Hill. There is just too much candy in the storefront, so before you know it, you are steaming down Sandy Point, across to Napatree, and heading for Watch Hill Harbor.

Little Naragansett Bay, as this whole area is called, underwent major reconstructive surgery during the hurricane of '38. The storm, dubbed The Long Island Express because of the speed and suddenness with which it approached from the southwest, hit Watch Hill mid afternoon on a sunny, humid, oppressive Wednesday in late September. R. A. Scotti has written a gripping account of this tragedy in her book *Sudden Sea.* No one was expecting it; there was no warning. The hurricane had threatened Florida a few days previously but was then downgraded, as it seemed to be moving northeasterly, further out to sea. It reappeared out of nowhere that Wednesday, thundering across Long Island toward Southeastern Connecticut and Rhode Island. Survivors spoke of a sound like a train and of seeing a thirty-foot-high wall of fog approaching. It was water they saw, not fog, but their minds could not accept that there could be water at that height. Those who were more than sixty feet from their homes when they first saw it could not run fast enough to get indoors before they were engulfed. The geography of the sandbars near Watch Hill was very different before the storm to what it is today. Sandy Point was joined to Napatree, and together with the mainland, they formed an idyllic rectangular-shaped lagoon, a small boaters' paradise. Napatree and Sandy Point were homes to a multitude of gracious summer cottages. The storm took all. Sandy Point was drastically rearranged into its current imprint and still moves around a bit with major storms.

I have heard stories that some wealthy families were able to evacuate to safety but left their immigrant, domestic help to perish. Scotti's book, on the other hand, details many extraordinary kindnesses, which families and servants gave to each other as they struggled together to live or die. I imagine that both stories are true. Who is to say what anyone of us would do if we were in peril of our lives? The final tally when the storm had passed and the dead were counted was that over four hundred souls perished in our short coastline as a result of this horrific storm.

***

The paddle down Sandy Point and across to Napatree is about two miles, and you can stay in shallow water if you plot your course well. The south side of Napatree is beautiful to walk but not quite as interesting to paddle except in high summer when it is crowded with boats. You will also come across a couple of small floating docks here with little shacks built on them and balconies up top! They really look very cute, at least when there are only a couple of them! The north side is more protected and is popular for sunbathing and swimming.

Watch Hill Yacht Club in high summer.

So we are drawn toward Watch Hill, around a little beach, and into the harbor. The village here feels as if it is frozen in time, I'm not sure when, but before my time. It's another, picture-perfect town with impressive homes on sloping hillsides, colorful stores, a working antique carousel, ice cream vendors, and a few restaurants. The Watch Hill Inn, a local eatery and landmark, sits on an incline facing the harbor. If you eat on the deck there, you can expect spectacular sunsets over the water. I highly recommend finding somewhere to beach, not at all an easy task, and wandering around the town for an hour. Another thing about Watch Hill is that, come Labor Day, it just zips itself up and hibernates. As full of life and as colorful as it is in summer, it is a lonely, windy ghost town in winter. And that's the way the locals like it. It takes all sorts!

To go farther east, you will need to go back around Napatree, a two-mile paddle, or you may be able to schlep your boat across the dunes as a short cut. I think I've done both. You need to be very careful if you go around Watch Hill Point. The rocks and reefs are treacherous here. It can be a lot of fun paddling the angry rips, but please take care; and don't go beyond your limits. The reward for your spirit of adventure is beautiful East Beach. This is the best public beach in a twenty- to fifty-mile radius. Public it is, but the natives don't make it easy. The main access from the land is a little rocky, hilly path between two mansions that winds four hundred feet down to the ocean. Once you get there, you see, on your left, a long golden Atlantic strand that ends in Misquamicut, the Rhode Island state beach. On your right is Watch Hill Point and Lighthouse, guarded by vertical black rocks and crashing waves. The beach is big enough, access too awkward and parking too complicated and expensive for it to ever get very crowded. Even on the major summer weekends, the crowds will congregate near the access points, so a couple of hundred yards' walk will give you plenty of space to spread out.

A couple of years back, I decided to drive out here in September to kayak in the surf. The waves here are classic Atlantic rollers, but there is quite an undertow; so swimmers need to be careful. Ocean View Highway is a pretty road that runs parallel to the beach for a couple of miles and is well worth a walk or drive. At the Watch Hill end, this road is lined with stately mansions, each one more dazzling than the next, including the pink "Bermuda House" and a striking Norman Castle–type dwelling. Hauling my kayak down the public access was not an attractive option for me, so I drove out Ocean View and found a lane running toward the beach, which dead-ended at the dunes. It was a beautiful, fresh day with great waves and a glorious sun. I took my Carolina off the car and headed straight for the water. Well, I must have been upended twenty times before I gave up and settled for a paddle farther out and parallel to the shore.

A Polynesian statue on the shore near Stony Creek
(Chapter 9).

If you ever try surf paddling, you'll find that you are at high risk of being turned and broached as you launch or beach. Plus, a sit-in, sea kayak will fill with water and sand every time. After my first attempts, it took a couple of months for the sand to fully work its way out of the rudder housing during which time lowering and raising it was awful. I talked Stuart into trying the surf here another year, but we ended up paddling to Watch Hill, as the sea was too calm that day. Next time I venture into heavy surf, I will rent a sit-on kayak so that upending is not a big deal.

I have never kayaked at Misquamicut. It's the state beach for Rhode Island, and it is densely packed in the summer. The strip here is becoming quite gentrified at each end and even in the middle. Fifteen years ago, this was like a border town; it felt wild and lawless. I think it's the first place I saw bars that fronted directly onto a beach.

***

Winnepaug Beach and Inn, and Quonochontaug Pond lie just beyond Misquamicut. It is a little known heavenly spot that is very easy to miss. Access to the beach here is very restricted. The most obvious route is just beyond Atlantic Avenue beside the Winnepaug Inn, but this is a private access for local residents only in the summer months. Some of these locals live in weathered, gabled cottages that sit on well-groomed commons or open heaths running down toward the water. The inn itself is very charming. Every other year, I will drive up there and walk around a bit if I'm not challenged, which I am usually not. It's a large, shingle-clad hotel behind the dunes, abutting the pond. It is very elegant and is patronized by fortunate families who rent rooms and suites for weeks at a time in the high season. It has big beautiful lawns and kayak and sailing facilities for residents. They have open-air picnics on the lawns on some Thursday evenings, and you can make reservations and join in.

Now that I've whetted your appetite, how can a yaker get on the water here? You ask. When in doubt, try Route 1. Although it's a mile inland, taking West Beach Road off the Old Post Road will bring you to a public access ramp on the east side of the pond. I launched here late one October to get in the last paddle of the year and also see the autumn leaves. I was wearing a thin, full-body wetsuit to keep warm and comfortable as my intention was to enjoy myself rather than do penance for my sins. This is a pretty, inland salt pond with the ubiquitous sea grasses and appealing homes scattered on its bank. I kayaked around it about two and a half miles and enjoyed the foliage with a small number of like-minded souls. As I moved west along the pond, a fog began to roll in, and the mood of the place changed from bright and colorful to muted and more mysterious. I did not realize that this was the salt pond that abutted the Winnepaug Inn until I came upon the establishment in question through the mist. This gave me my bearings, so I landed and dragged my boat over the dunes in the fog, and like "Stout Cortez," "silent upon a peak in Darien," I took in the beautiful Atlantic beach and waves. Moments like these are wonderful little adventures and discoveries for the ordinary person. I was so moved by the experience that I raced down the clean sand and plunged headfirst into the waves for a refreshing swim. At least I think I did, or I may have, or I would have if the water were not freezing!

Looking back at the journeys that I have described in this chapter, I realize that they cover about twenty-five miles as an out and back. Since I have described it as a single trip, it's only fair to mention that you can split it into two, or more, separate day trips. Whichever way you want to divide it up, the Tuesday Night Paddlers put-in's are a nice way of experiencing some or all of it.

9

Dancing in the Dark

(Sunset over Stonington. Upriver at night. Thimble Islands by moonlight. A beer in Watch Hill. Gazing at the skies.)

There are few pursuits that I can think of that can be enjoyed outdoors in the dark. I'm thinking of sporting pursuits, so please control your imagination! Paddling in the dark is a lot of fun and much less demanding than you might think. My first encounters with night-time paddling were with the Tuesday-night group. Every four weeks or so, the schedule would include a full-moon paddle.

One that I remember fondly started out from Quiambaug Cove around six in the evening and headed for Sandy Point. It was a large group, and we made good time to the point where we beached facing the back of Stonington Borough. Out came the sandwiches and snacks with sodas or beer, and we sat around munching and chatting. The sun began to set about eight, and the light took on that pink or purple hue that is so magical. The roofs and gables of the houses in the borough stood out in dark silhouette against the flaming sky. When we looked toward Watch Hill, it appeared as if one of the big buildings on the hill was on fire. This was the Yellow House, which is a large, old wooden hotel (now being recreated) on a cliffs above East Beach. The sunset over Stonington was reflecting on the many windows of the hotel in a rich, golden blaze of glory. I remember a fragment from *The Wind in the Willows* where someone (probably Ratty) was totally overcome by the splendor and majesty of a beautiful sunrise. Our experience that evening was somewhat similar. We lingered there in awe for a long time, our heads swinging from the borough to Watch Hill and back trying to drink in all of the panoramic scene. Even after the sun had fully set, the Yellow House was still illuminated, either because of its elevation or some bending of the solar rays. We ended our evening paddling contentedly back to Quiambaug Cove, still enveloped in the aura of a lovely dusk.

You need to take some extra precautions when you are on the water after dark. I prefer not to be alone out there, in general. Also, navigation is much more challenging, and it's best to be able to see well-lit, familiar landmarks or be accompanied by an experienced guide. You really need at least two lights, fore and aft, either on your flotation jacket or affixed to the boat. There is nothing worse than paddling along, without lights, listening to the roar of a powerboat approaching at high speed from behind. There are a variety of battery-operated, waterproof lights available at boating and hardware stores. Finally, night-time paddling is best restricted to favorable weather conditions.

An evening trip I like to take at least once every year is from Masons Island to the Mystic Seaport and back. This one I will do alone as it is pretty sheltered, and you can stay close to the shore most of the time. It's a little adventure, reminiscent perhaps of the British foray up the river in 1812. You pass quietly under the railroad bridge and paddle past the large powerboats that line this stretch of the river. At weekends, you will hear subdued voices from dimly lit craft and sometimes an entertainer or singer in the Daniel Packer Inn. You are occasionally surprised by the clear voice of someone sitting at the stern of a boat, or indeed, you may give them a start. The lighting is better near the Mystic Drawbridge, and you will often see young lovers caressing either on the wooden boardwalk or on the lawn of the Art Association. Up under the bridge and on toward the Seaport, you glide silently amongst the historic whaling ships that are docked there. It's a great little trip, and you get caught up in the atmosphere and beauty of it all.

***

Karen and I had a different type of night-time excursion at the Thimble Islands last September. As a birthday gift, she treated me to a night at an unlikely but charming B&B, near the water just outside of downtown New Haven. We dined elegantly at the old Charthouse at Oyster Point and then headed off for a guided, moonlight tour of the Thimble Islands. Stony Creek village boat ramp, near Branford, provides convenient access to the islands, and we drove over there after dinner. There was a good fifteen- to twenty-knot wind blowing that evening, which worried me a lot, and my fears were not diminished when we saw whitecaps near the shore as we arrived at Ferry Point after dark. Karen is a good beginner paddler, but I was afraid that the conditions might be too demanding for her. I also had some previous experience of challenging tidal currents around here. Against my better judgment, I kept my fears to myself. I was very touched by the thoughtfulness of her gift and did not want to spoil it. Our guide, Rich, was at the boat ramp with a small selection of boats, as were another couple who were also supposed to be taking the tour. They had brought their own boats, which were short, squat and not designed for spray skirts. It also transpired that they were both beginners.

After a short, private pow-wow, they decided not to go out with us, which did not help my confidence a lot.

Karen had built me up as a master kayaker to Rich, so he assigned me a long slim sleek hot-rod with a skeg but no rudder. "The boat will track better without a rudder," he lied shamelessly. Ya, right! Karen got a slightly more stable boat but again with no rudder. Immediately, we headed out; we felt the challenge. The wind was on our left as were the rolling waves. The water felt cold, and the darkness did not help either. Rich, of course, set a very brisk pace, which we tried to match. I had a hell of a time keeping on course with the wind and waves trying to turn me and needing to paddle double strokes on my right to try and stay straight. I can't remember if I tried to edge the boat to steer it, probably not. I did let down the skeg, however, or at least I tried to let it down. When we finally got back to land, Rich nonchalantly informed me that the skeg mechanism was not working. In the first half mile, I must have come close to overturning a dozen times, and I can only imagine how Karen stayed upright.

I took matters into my own hands eventually and declared that we would be more comfortable if we paddled into the wind, parallel to and near the shore. This worked out very well, and we got a good stroke going as we headed east and enjoyed the sights of the warmly lit coastal homes on our left. We turned in due course and headed west toward the little islands. I don't know this area well, but on the charts, it looks like there are about twenty islands ranging from five acres to a few hundred square yards. We really began to enjoy ourselves on this leg. Many of the islands have unique homes on their shores, some of them residences of famous celebrities. One islet was little more than a fifty-by-forty-square-yard rock, jutting out of the water. It had a flat, low-roofed house perched high on it's crown and was brightly illuminated with spotlights. Just by the front door was a V-shaped, stone passageway with steps leading down to the water. At the bottom of the steps, to our surprise, an athletic-looking young man, clad in a swimsuit, emerged from a steaming Jacuzzi which was nestled in the rocks. At that same instant, an extravagant fireworks display exploded about five miles away, on the mainland, and lit up the night sky behind the house. I assumed that all of this was laid on for my birthday, but Karen's sarcastic chuckle suggested not. It would be hard to better a visual feast like this, so after our customary "but are these people really happy?" discussion, we headed back. We nearly upended again a couple of times as we came close to the shore. I am sure that the treachery of these waters must be very familiar to local kayakers. They also have a curious means of mooring boats out here using narrow, upright stakes that are driven into the mud. Karen bumped into one of these and nearly went over, but luckily, our guide was able to pull her back upright. This was very fortunate as a cold dousing, and a difficult, wet reentry in the dark would have taken the gloss off of what turned out to be a great little adventure.

***

One evening, last autumn, John and I planned to kayak from Dubois Beach as a change from our frequent Mystic River jaunts. I was late in arriving, I think; my old station wagon would not start. By the time John picked me up and we got to the beach, the sun was already setting. It was a lovely evening, and quite a number of people were congregated there, some with wine and snacks, to watch the sun go down. There was also a group of scuba divers popping up and down just off the beach. It felt strange to be heading out when everyone one else was packing up, but it was still warm; and the sky had that beautiful pink glow. We paddled off toward Sandy Point at a brisk pace chatting like crazy as we had not seen each other for a while. It seemed to take an awful long time to get even close to Sandy Point until John pointed out that we had bypassed it completely and were closing in on the tip of Napatree. By this time, dusk had passed and darkness had set in.

One of the nice things about this part of Little Naragansett Bay is that it is quite shallow, so you don't need to worry too much about powerboats. We steamed west, parallel to the beach, toward Watch Hill Harbor passing a little sailboat that had pulled its anchor and run aground on the sand, lying on its side in the moonlight. This is a good little paddle, about a mile and a half. As I've mentioned elsewhere, I love entering quaint little harbors, and Watch Hill is one of my favorites. It was about eight thirty, and I had the bright idea of beaching at the yacht club and having a beer. This we did and had no difficulty in wangling our way in and getting served. We limited ourselves to the one, and a beer never tasted so good.

The journey back to Stonington Point was about three miles, but the evening was warm, the seas calm; and we had a bright moon to light our way, which was comforting. As we neared the harbor, we had a bit of an argument as to which was the light emanating from the lighthouse at the Point. John's choice proved to be off by half a mile, but since I don't rub it in when I am, frequently, right, it didn't detract from a lovely evening.

***

If I could roll all of our night-time paddles into one, archetypal example, it would be a night in high summer a couple of years ago. We had been out for a couple of hours and ended up near Ram Island, at the mouth of the Mystic River, as the evening fell. The moon was full and bright. It was that year when Mars, I think, was very close to Earth and was clearly visible as a large, orange star. We rounded Enders and headed up the east side of Masons Island. The waves were lapping on the rocks and, up ahead, we could see soft, yellow lights in the windows of the yacht club. It was a holiday time, and there were a couple of large sailboats and cruisers docked at the club with little groups socializing on board whose voices could be heard across the still water. We dallied near the yacht club and turned east to gaze at the moon, which was low in the sky with the red planet resplendent above it. In the far distance, we could see the flickering of the lighthouse on Block Island, high on the bluffs about twenty miles away. We moved slowly toward the causeway pausing every now and then to look back at the skies. We were still not ready to call it a day when we reached the Mystic River, so we made a run up to the seaport, and only then did we reluctantly head for home.

10

Fishers Island

(Rich millionaires and poor millionaires. West Harbor. Dave and the buddy system. In amongst the spinnakers. Golfing on the water. Plum Island.)

Most of the kayaking I have been describing takes place in Fishers Island Sound, and this island is a striking, visual presence a lot of the time that we spend on the water. Through the tricks of light and perspective, it sometimes looms very large from the mainland and at other times seems quite distant. Geographically, it is about five miles long and ranges from a couple of hundred yards to a mile in width. It's a stringy sort of an island, two to three miles from the coast and pointing toward Watch Hill. Curiously, it is "in" New York state although its only ferry comes out of New London, and it must be ten miles at least from Long Island. The demographics are best summed up by a description I once heard: "The rich millionaires live on the east end of the island, and the poor millionaires live at the other end." I took the ferry out there one Saturday before I began kayaking. I have always loved visiting islands, big or small, near or far. They all tend to

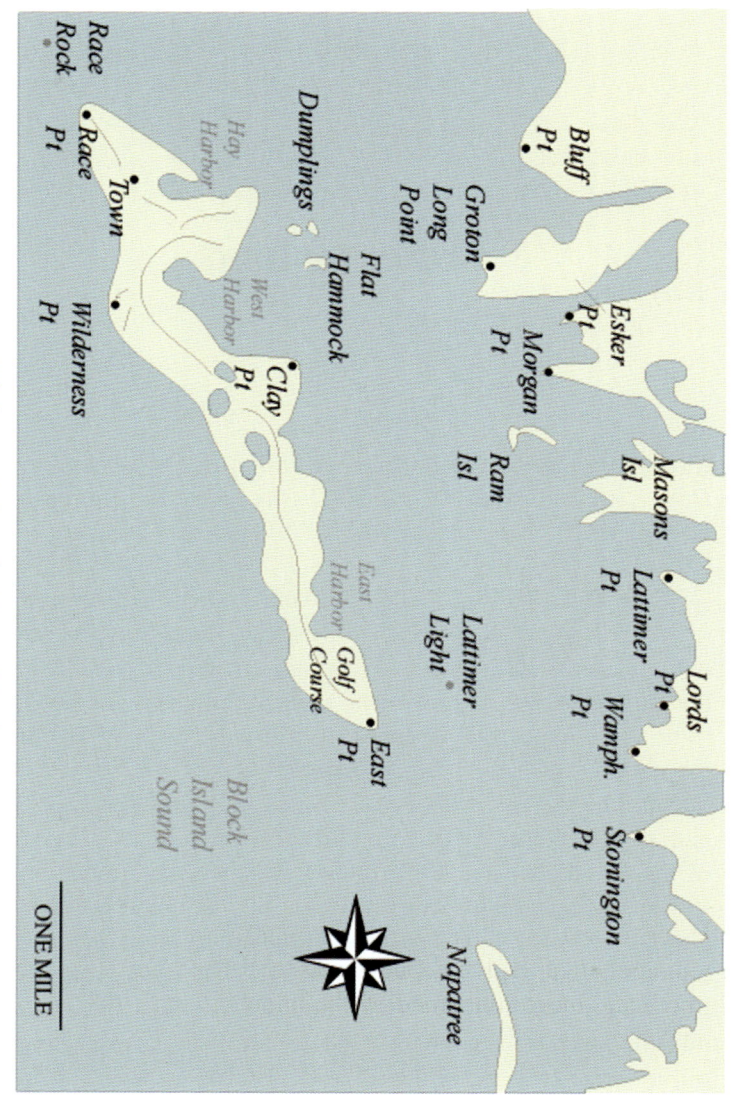

Fishers Island, New York

have a unique personality, and they can be very idiosyncratic. Then there is the boat journey, in this case a modest car ferry but still fun in good weather. The ferry docks in Hay Harbor and disgorges its passengers there. The day I visited, my plan was to walk the length of the island. I soon discovered though that about a third of the way along, the road becomes private and is guarded by a security shack. This shack was not manned, so I wandered on but eventually, feeling a bit out of place on the lonely roads, I retraced my steps. I settled instead for a ramble on the southern beaches and circled back to the ferry by the shore.

The first time John and I kayaked to Fishers was supposed to be with the Paddlers. We had made an informal arrangement with Stan, Bill, and a couple of others to paddle out there on a Saturday morning. This felt like a major journey, and John suggested that we take his double kayak. That way, if one of us had difficulties, the other could bring us home. The idea made sense to me, and it worked out fine. The morning of the big day dawned to a thick fog. Our agreed-upon meeting place was Esker Point beach in Noank, and when we arrived, there were only three others, Bill and his nephew and another friend, Dave. Visibility was under fifty yards, and it was obvious that we could not set out unless the fog lifted. While we waited, we headed to Carson's Store in Noank for a coffee. Carson's is a quaint old ice cream parlor, café, and store with a couple of round, tubular stools beside a Formica marble counter, a great place to have a coffee or snack and catch up on the local gossip. Noank Village itself is very pretty with its beautiful Baptist church right at the top of Main Street. As we lounged around and chatted, it slowly emerged that Bill's nephew was a novice and was getting more and more concerned by the minute about our trip. In the end, he and Bill wisely decided to save this adventure for another day.

Although it felt like it was never going to do so, the fog eventually lifted enough for us to see about half a mile and

Dave, John, and I headed out into the sound. If visibility stayed as it was or even deteriorated, we could navigate home by compass. Dave is a funny fellow. He must be about sixty, midsize, lean, and muscular with a bald pate and a roguish smile. He is a very strong paddler and can easily leave me in his wake. He is always play-acting at one thing or another, sprinting ahead, practicing bracing, or doing half-Eskimo rolls. Well, the trip out went fine. It was a bit spooky at first, setting out in the fog without being able to see our destination. But, by the time we had reached the halfway point, visibility had improved enough such that we could see both Esker Point

The narrow strip of sand in West Harbor where we beach on Fishers Island.

and the island, and a warm sun was beginning to burn through. Our destination was West Harbor, which lines up approximately with Mumford Cove on the mainland. The outer harbor is a good size and very pretty with coastal homes scattered sparsely on the shores. One house has a long lawn and a seawall with a small beach on the water's edge. The kids, I presume, who live there have painted the slogan "Where the Wild Ones Live" on the wall, in large colorful letters, which is pretty cute.

One of the challenges the island presents to the paddler is that it is a very private place. While the perimeter of the harbor must be two miles in length, there is almost nowhere to land that is not designated as private. This includes the small, town beach. We found a little spit of sand on the west side of the harbor, near the yacht club, and were able to pull our boats out there. Out came the ham sandwiches and the sodas, and for about ten minutes, there was mostly silence, ending with contented sighs. Just before we began to explore farther, a group of about ten kayakers pulled up beside us and began their picnic. In response to a query as to where they had come from, we learned that the whole group had just paddled over from Montauk, which is about ten miles away! I was flabbergasted at this, as a twenty-mile round-trip would take me seven hours at least. Since then I have met what I would call ultra-kayakers one of whom claimed, and I believe him, to have paddled from Stonington to Block Island to Montauk and back all in one day. That's got to be forty to fifty miles!

The walk from West Harbor to the town center is about a mile or so and a pleasant diversion. The narrow roadways are pretty quiet with a few houses, a craft shop, and some market gardens on the way. Whenever you pass someone, they say hello, but you feel that they must know that you are not a local. I really like the village green. It's encircled with a few shops, a small café, and the town library, and it is a lovely place to lounge on a warm summer afternoon.

Eventually, we headed back to the harbor not wanting to be paddling home too late in the day. John and I were a little slow in getting going, launching in a double requires a little extra care. By the time we had put-in, Dave had paddled five hundred yards out into the harbor and was still accelerating. I should point out that before we headed out in the morning we had all sworn an oath that we would stay together since there were only two boats involved. We paddled along fully expecting that Dave would slow down so that we could join him. The opposite was the case. He was paddling like a fury, and we quickly lost sight of him. Since then I have taken up scuba diving where the buddy system is one of the cornerstones of safety in this sport. They have a term for irresponsible diving partners called "same-ocean buddies" meaning that the only thing that is guaranteed is that your buddy is in the same general body of water.

We became more and more upset with our "buddy" as we paddled along. Firstly, he could not come to our aid if we needed help. More scary, though, the seas were three to four feet, and since we could not see him, we were not sure if he was OK. The specter of returning home, and having to report that we did not know where our friend was, weighed heavily on us. We did what we could, zigzagging a bit, shouting, etc., to connect with him, but it was not until we got close to land that we spotted him about half a mile to our right. We gave him a hard time of it when we got ashore, but it just ran off him.

***

The second time I kayaked to Fishers was with a large armada of the Paddlers. Stuart and I set out from the Mystic River expecting to join the flotilla as it came out from Eskers and past Morgan Point. By the time we reached the sound, the greyhounds were well out of the trap, and the fleet was a third of the way across. We paddled hard to catch up and eventually joined the stragglers as they beached on Flat Hammock, a hundred-yard-long spit of sand that is only exposed at low tide. Nearby here are the two Dumpling Islands, one of which is a home to Dean Kamen, the inventor of the Segway Transporter, complete with lighthouse,

100

windmill, amphibious vehicle, and helipad. Our group was pretty large, over thirty boats, and it must have been an impressive sight when we entered West Harbor and crowded onto the only non-private bit of sand available. We wandered up toward the village, a disheveled gaggle of men and women in shorts and flip-flops, some still wearing flotation vests, something akin to a Viking invasion. Local residents gave us some curious glances as we passed by.

A sloop, close-hauled, near Fishers Island

Our group congregated on the green and enjoyed a picnic in the warm sun. Another challenge on private islands is finding the toilets when they are needed. One of our number had local knowledge and led us to a well-hidden public loo. The day was saved! Before we headed for home, we paddled deep into West Harbor. It is a pretty little backwater to explore if you have the time.

The paddle home was exciting. The seas and wind were challenging but manageable. It was a Saturday in the height of summer, hot and sunny, and there were hundreds of boats on the water from Niantic to Watch Hill. As we made our way back, we crossed the course of a sailboat race. There was a strong breeze, and the thirty-foot sloops were steaming along very close to our boats. Just where our paths intersected, the sailboats were rounding a marker buoy, lowering their head sails and hoisting spinnakers. It was very colorful and exciting, the whoosh of the boats as they cut through the chop and the bark of the kites as they inflated. As I mentioned, the day was very warm, and by the time we made it back to Mystic, we were tired and dehydrated. It was still only midafternoon however, so plenty of time to relax and recover.

***

Another long journey that we have thought about is to circumnavigate Fishers Island. At first glance, it does not seem to be a big deal, relative to Block or Montauk, but when you get out the tape measure, you discover that it's a twenty to twenty-five–mile trip. As well as that, the waters at both ends of the island are extremely challenging, and the south side faces the open Atlantic. One day last year, John and I set out to sail around Fishers. I have a 1980's Pearson 26, which is a solid, seaworthy craft although the cockpit arrangement is somewhat awkward. Up to this trip, I had stayed within the confines of Fishers Island Sound, mainly influenced by the time it takes to sail any farther and by my lack of knowledge farther out.

Long Island Sound is guarded at its eastern end by Montauk and Napatree, but an awful lot of its tidal flow is funneled toward Fishers by Orient Point and Plum Island. The tidal currents here are very strong, and there are legendary reefs and ledges, which produce awesome rips. On the day in question, with a good fifteen-knot breeze from the north, we sailed briskly out to Latimer Light and then steered carefully through the reef-strewn passage between Watch Hill and Fishers. This is a favorite spot for fishermen, and you will often see little flotillas in the area. A neighbor of mine was fishing here with friends one weekend in a twenty-foot Boston Whaler in rough seas. Their boat was suddenly swamped, and they were all dumped in the drink. The water temperature was in the fifties, and help was not quick in coming. They bound themselves together with ropes and were contemplating what seemed like an inevitable end when they were luckily spotted and rescued by a passing boat.

As we rounded the eastern point of the island, the Pearson began to purr along in a lively beam breeze. The seas were four to five feet, but our craft felt very steady. We ate our sandwiches as we cruised along enjoying the sights, the lovely homes, and the beaches. Fishers Island boasts an outstanding, links golf course that runs down to the water on both sides at the east end of the island. Every time I catch a glimpse of it, I resolve to play there someday if I can wangle an invite. There is also a smaller, nine-hole course on the south-western shore and this very pretty as well.

Near the western tip are Valiant Rock and Race Rock and the Gull Islands where huge, underwater canyons plunge suddenly from twenty to three hundred feet causing furious rips when the waters of Long Island Sound are driven through by the tides. This is also a very popular fishing spot, and blues abound here. The first time I experienced "the race," as these rips are called, was in a small powerboat while fishing with a neighbor. I was truly horrified by the chaotic power of the waves and scared of my life of drifting back into them. Luckily, my friend knew what he was doing, so no harm ensued.

From this commentary, you will not be surprised that we went out of our way to give the race a wide berth before we turned and sailed back to Mystic. One other curiosity of note in this area is Plum Island, which lines up with Fishers but is much closer to Orient Point. This is home to a United States government, veterinary infectious-disease laboratory. The island has been immortalized in the DeMille novel of the same name and in a recent expose probing its role in developing biological weapons. This latter book also develops a theory that Lyme disease originated here from an inadvertent leak of viral agents.

To conclude with Fishers Island, another paddle that I would like to take is from Mystic to East Harbor. I have sailed out there a couple of times, and it's very pretty; but I could never get too close for fear of rocks. You can see the golf course from the water here. One of the fairways, which always seems to be a deep, verdant green color slopes down to the sea with majestic trees on either side. I'm hoping that there is a little beach where one can land. A little trip to look forward to!

11

Further Afield

*(Newport, Rhode Island. The wild man who ran the
breachway. Pleasant but not Friendly.)*

There is a wealth of beautiful kayaking where we live in Southeastern Connecticut and, because of this, not a lot of motivation to look farther afield. I tend to be opportunistic in trying out other locations. For example, last year Karen and I spent two nights in Newport, Rhode Island, and I took advantage of the opportunity to kayak the harbor there. Most large, coastal towns now have at least one rental location. One of these in Newport is right downtown, off Water Street. For twenty-five bucks, you can rent a boat for a couple of hours and launch off of a little beach. There is an awful lot to see here, megayachts, America's Cup beauties, and the famous mansions from the water to mention but a few. The New York Yacht Club has a beautiful manor here with a long lawn running down to a sandy beach. Attendants were raking the sand as I paddled by! I asked if I could pull in for a chat and a pint and a sandwich, but they never really seemed to warm up to the idea. There are also some beautiful little coves with pretty houses atop small cliffs that must be a joy to live in. As you go out the east shore, you will come upon Fort Adams, which is famous for its music festivals. It was here in 1965 that Bob Dylan thumbed his nose at his folk followers and began his legendary rock and roll career.

I made the crossing from Fort Adams back to Goat Island, but I would advise a lot of caution if you choose to do this. It's pretty exposed out there with an awful lot of boat traffic and strong currents. I see that the Paddlers now have a trip from Fort Wetherill in Jamestown to Newport on their schedule, and I hope to take advantage of this next year.

The waters around Wickford Harbor are also very interesting, and you can rent boats there at the Kayak Center and also take courses and guided tours to familiarize yourself with kayaking and the local waters. They really have a great setup with a sheltered pond for learning strokes, a delightful picnic spot beside their training center, a nearby beach to practice exits, rescues, rolls, and an exposed bay for open-water and rock-play experience.

***

A bit closer to home, Ninigret Pond is an interesting place to paddle if you want a mixture of calm and adventure. I wandered up there on my own one Saturday and had a hell of a day out. The only access I was able to find was off of Route 1 and down some lanes to a marina. The road dead-ends at the marina, and you are left scratching your head looking for the public boating access. It's actually right in front of you! What looks like a muddy drain is the designated put in. For such a beautiful spot, the access is less than promising. As always, things improve once you are on the water. You head south in a cove for about three quarters of a mile flanked on both sides by marsh grasses and foliage. Once you exit the cove, you are in a four-mile-by-two-mile, expansive salt pond. The scene here on a summer weekend is a bit of a tonic.

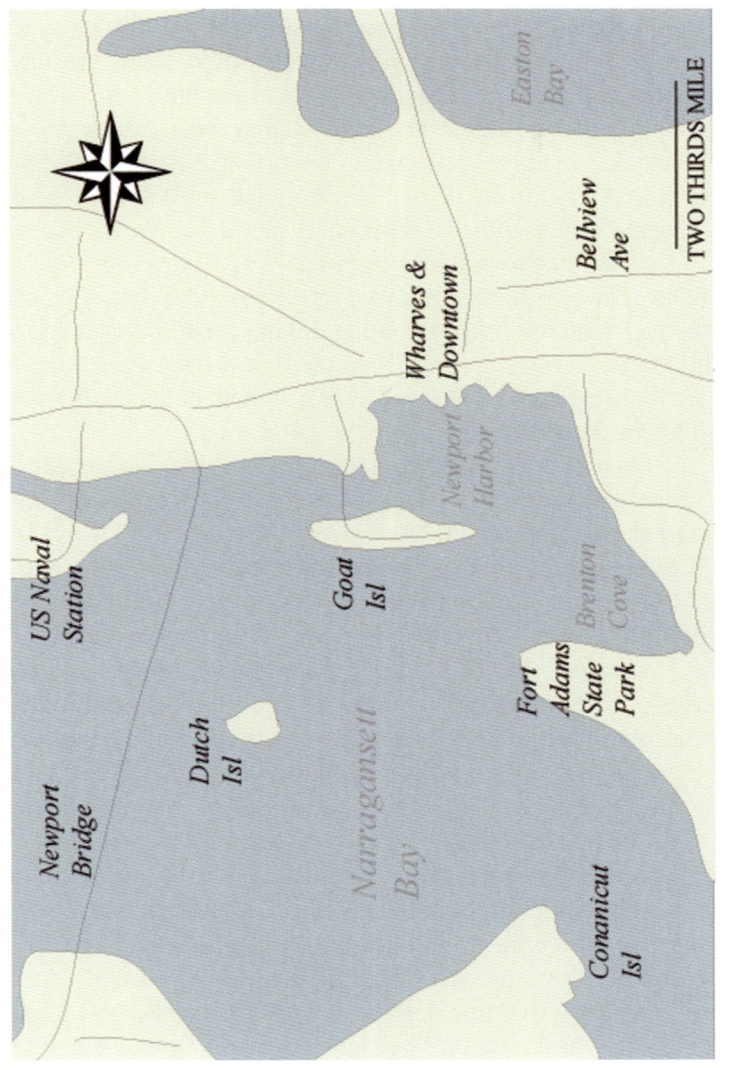

Newport Harbor, Rhode Island

There are clammers everywhere. The shallow waters are ideal for this pursuit. I would guess that there were a couple of hundred people scattered all over, in sailboats, Lasers, jet skis, kayaks, and pretty much anything that would float, the day that I visited here. I headed diagonally across the pond toward an area where the largest group of boaters was congregated. This led me toward a little canal, again with lots of activities in its waters and on its banks. I rested and took in the sights as I floated along with the current. I met a couple of yakers after a while and inquired as to what was farther on. They replied, "Oh, we're not allowed go down that far," which seemed a bit quaint as they were strapping men and women in their twenties. In retrospect, I realize that the reason for their restriction was that they were using rented boats, and their cautious instructions were from the rental shop.

On I floated, and the current got appreciably faster. As I rounded the last bend at a fair pace, I caught my first sight of the sea about two hundred yards away. This was the point of no return. A more prudent person would, and could, have turned and backtracked here if they acted quickly and paddled hard. But I did not. That split second was gone, and I went careening forward into what I now know is the Charleston Breachway. This is where the full ten square miles of tidal salt pond gushes out through a narrow channel and hits the incoming tide. Everything happened very quickly then. I was conscious of people fishing on both sides, casting into the rip from the raised banks and rocks. It occurred to me, briefly, that there was some danger to me in this, but by that time, I was heading into ferocious seas (for a kayaker) where the ebbing and incoming waters met. The waves were huge and were coming at me crazily from different directions. I felt a sharp tug on my flotation vest, which I later learned was a big fishing lure, but the nylon line snapped easily leaving the lure hooked on the vest as a momento. One instinct that serves us well in situations like this is to paddle furiously. It gives you forward momentum, and also your paddle is never too long

A quiet backwater in Essex, Ct.

out of the water on either side, which allows you to brace when needed. I wish I could say that I survived the breachway, but in reality, it just spat me out when it was done with me. By luck, I was able to stay afloat as I barely escaped overturning with each stroke until, eventually, I was beyond the turmoil no more than a hundred yards from the shore. I felt elated after this adventure into which I had been involuntarily drafted.

When the euphoria wore off, I realized that I had another problem to deal with, how to get back to the pond and, thereby, my station wagon? Scanning the beaches on both sides gave no hint of a calmer inlet. So I braced myself and paddled hard, back into the fray. I tried this twice, but on both occasions, I was spat back out. Eventually, I settled for beaching and hauling my boat over the dunes and back into the canal. As I paddled back, a group of teenagers hailed me as "the wild man who ran the breachway." Respect at last.

***

The Paddlers are a great group with which to get to know different venues. With them, John, Stuart, and I have paddled the waters around Niantic Bay including Millstone and Seaside Point (yes, we do glow in the dark now!) on the east side of the bay and Black Point on the west side. We spent one Saturday morning at Great Island in Old Lyme improving our rescue and rolling skills although I have to say that we were bitten a lot by large nasty horseflies.

John has taken a big liking to the Connecticut River, and he now has good local knowledge of it. I've paddled there with him a couple of times, once in Lords Cove, which is spectacular in its natural beauty, and once in Hamburg Cove, which is equally attractive but in a different way. I've also boated, but not kayaked, farther upriver, and the waters around Essex are very interesting. Undoubtedly, this river, which is 400 miles long and rises near the Canadian

110

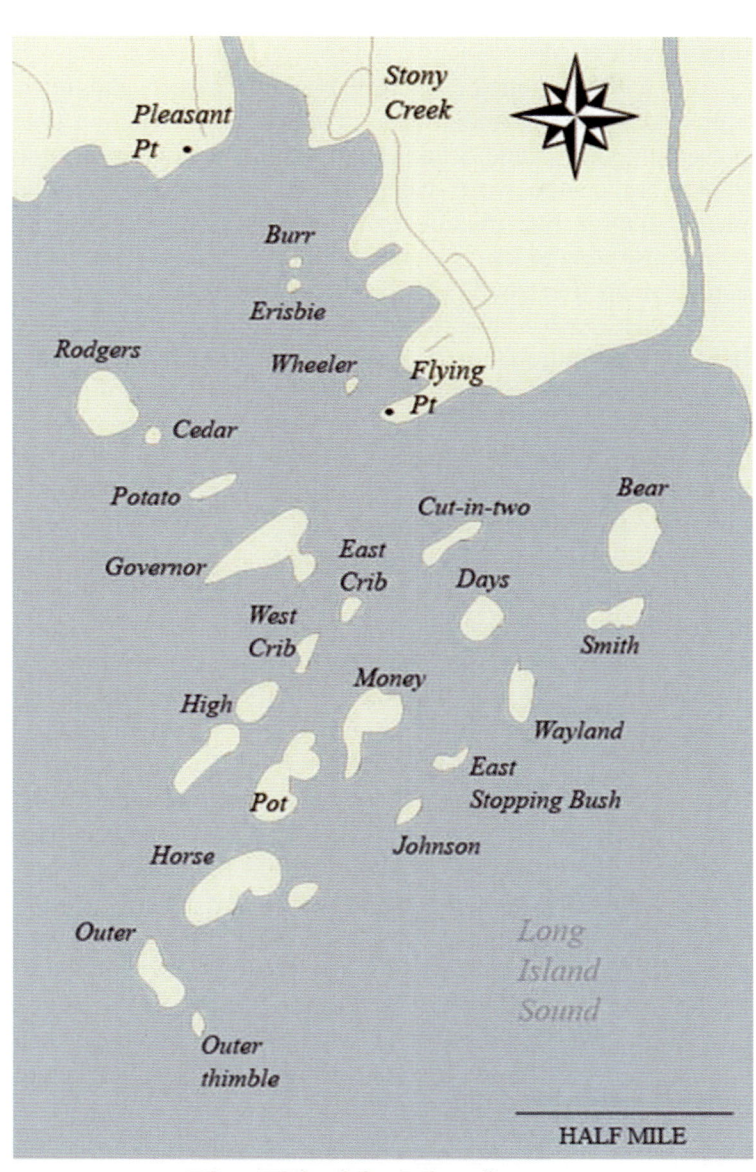

The Thimble Islands

border, must be a vast, Pandora's box of wonderful paddling opportunities.

I've mentioned the Thimble Islands earlier, and this is a great daytime destination also. One of the islands is a state preserve (Outer Island, I think) and has big flat ledges of pink granite beside the water where you can lie in the sun and picnic. I think that picnicking there may be frowned upon, which just adds to the enjoyment. But, please be responsible and clean up after you if you do venture out here.

Although I have never paddled out to Block Island (it is approx. 10 miles from the Connecticut-Rhode Island shore), I have kayaked while visiting there. On one occasion, when we were over-nighting on a friend's boat, I borrowed one of their small Daggers to explore the Great Salt Pond where we were moored. This is a well-protected body of water, the only outlet being the narrow channel that connects to the open ocean. The surroundings here are interesting and colorful in the summer. The town has rental moorings, which are in great demand and local marinas run frequent shuttles to bring sailors ashore. There are a couple of enjoyable features for the paddler. One is to meander on the western shore and check out the distinctive homes that are planted there. Continuing further north will bring you to the narrow harbor entrance where it is exciting to sunbathe and watch the marine traffic come and go. At the eastern shore, the pond is only separated from the Atlantic by a thin sliver of road and dunes. You can beach here and walk across to the ocean to swim. Another great way to experience the island is to rent a bike and cycle the perimeter roads. It's pretty hilly, but well worth the effort. Once you get out of the town the natural beauty is unspoiled. There are miles of winding, hilly roads flanked with green fields and occasional, shimmering salt ponds and narrow cow-paths leading down to the sea.

Back in 1998, John passed on a *New York Times* article to me on kayaking from inn to inn in coastal Maine. The author waxed lyrical, as authors will, about the beauty of

Friendship, Maine

the coastline and memories of beaching on lawns of historic inns at the close of a strenuous day's paddling. I seem to remember that there was also mention of sumptuous, home-cooked meals and after-dinner drinks on porches overlooking the ocean. I get taken-in by hype like this a lot although I am definitely improving with age. I decided to combine a late September, extended weekend of golf in Vermont with some friends from work with a road trip to Maine. The golf was to commence Friday and end on Sunday at which time I headed east in the general direction of Camden, Maine. If you ever try to drive east across the upper New England states, you will quickly discover that all of the major roads run north-south, which makes for a long journey. After a couple of hours driving in the late afternoon, I overnighted in some motel-Hitchcock in a nondescript town and continued my journey the next morning.

My destination was a little village called Friendship, which is on a deep inlet between Boothbay Harbor and Rockland and near a headland called Pleasant Point. I stayed at an inn on the harbor, which was a bright, agreeable place and also home to what looked like a pretty serious kayaking school. Unfortunately, it was very much the end of the season, and there were no other kayakers around. So you could say that it was a pleasant but not overly friendly experience! In fact, the whole trip felt kind of lonely and end of year-ish. I did have some memorable paddles however. One was around what I believe is Friendship Island and peeking out into Muscongus Bay. The weather was glorious, but the water was cold; and there was a brisk breeze. I have to admit that I felt pretty exposed and fragile out there, much more than I do in Fishers Island Sound.

On another day, I drove to Rockport to put in there and paddled to Camden. This whole area is a big beneficiary of a major finance company's philanthropy and, as a result, Rockport has several excellent art museums devoted to the work of Andrew Wyeth and his family. It was a treat for me to visit there, as I have always liked the remote and forlorn atmospheres that Wyeth's paintings evoke. The paddle from Rockport to Camden is about five miles, but again, I would advise against doing this alone as I did. There are several distinct parts to this trip. You begin by traveling south, down Rockport Harbor, then round a point to head for Camden. On this leg of the journey, you are flanked on your left by high, rocky shores topped with a thick curtain of stately evergreens. Very different from the Connecticut shoreline, which seems more interesting to me as you can see much more without the trees.

Finally, you turn and head into Camden Harbor, which is a real treat. It's a bustling, colorful waterway with a potpourri of waterside restaurants, each with a great view of the hillside town and its verdant green running down to the water. I beached near the town green and spent a couple of happy hours wandering around the streets before heading back to sea. While my experiences in this area did not equal the newspapers' hype (it never does!), I imagine that it is glorious in the high summer and would recommend a paddle out of Camden if you are in the area.

Beyond these experiences in the northeast, I have only kayaked in a couple of other areas in the United States such as Clearwater in Florida and Seabrook Island in South Carolina, so the opportunities to explore farther are vast!

The "50-s" List

That about completes this little book on kayaking. One of the things I have enjoyed in writing it is pulling out the charts to check place-names and realizing that even very close to home I have been blowing by some interesting-looking inlets in my hurry to get to the next great spot. Sometimes we need to go slower to see more, rather than travel farther or faster.

John tells a story of a friend who, when he turned the half century, decided to make a list of fifty fun things that he wanted to do in his life going forward. I have never been that hot on lists in planning for my future, and over the years, I trust more and more that life will play itself out in its own interesting way. Having said all of this, I do find this "50" list interesting, conceptually at least. I mentioned this to Karen recently and asked her what she would put on her list. She quickly answered that holding her son's firstborn in her arms would fit the bill for her, which just underlines that women are wise, men are idiots, and we are unbelievably lucky that any good woman will take us on!

There are places to kayak that I would put on my list; narrow mountain lakes in Vermont, San Diego harbor, and the La Jolla coastline. I would imagine that coastal Washington and Oregon must be awesome. Likewise, the East Coast, inland waterways in the summer, or a paddle around the island of Manhattan! In England, a trip up the Thames to Henley and Oxford would be mighty, and the whole Scottish coastline must be stunning. Then one could try places like Lake Geneva, the Seine, Venice, if allowed. And, of course, the rivers, lakes and coastline of my homeland, Ireland. The list is endless but, as a much-maligned Irish parliamentarian once asked about posterity, what did lists ever do for me?

The sailboat "Brilliant" at the Mystic Seaport.

Let's forget the lists and think instead of the enjoyment that can be experienced on small, safe journeys in whatever area we live in or find ourselves visiting. No great planning or preparation is required. Just drop the boats, your own or rentals, in the water, and off you go. If we live life with a zest, we will be ready for winter when it comes. One of the earliest Paddlers' schedule that I came across listed the final destination of the year as Bangor, Maine. At first, I thought that this was an ambitious late-season road trip but then realized it was just the author's way of saying that it was time to put the boats away for the year and turn our minds to other things like Thanksgiving, Christmas, the cold and the snow and the long winter and spring of the northeast. So in that spirit, I will bid you adieu and hope that our paths may cross, and we will share a story or two in April or May on the beautiful waters of Fishers Island Sound.

If you enjoyed this book, you can order additional copies at www.kayakmysticwaters.com.

Notes and References

1. The Mystic River
   1. The Mystic Community Center (MCC). Now renamed as Mystic YMCA. I prefer the older name! Note that permission from the Y may be required to launch from the beach in summer months

   2. Indian Graves. "A House Gives Way to Sacred Ground," New York Times, Sunday, November 7, 2004.

   3. War of 1812. *"The Battle of Stonington: Torpedoes, Submarines and Rockets in the war of 1812"* by James Tertius De Kay, 1990. My comments in this book were gleaned from a lecture that I heard the author give in Dodson's Boatyard in Stonington and a reading of his book!

   4. Morgan Point Lighthouse. *Coastal Living Magazine*, November-December 1999.

2. Masons Island
   1. Pequot Indians and Masons Island. *"Major John Mason's Great Island"* by James H. Allyn, 1976. Allyn's father and uncle bought the island after the death of one the last of the Mason's (Andrew) in 1912.

   2. Shields are a one-design class sailboat. There are several fleets that race in the area. The boats are very attractive, overhung, fast, and sleek.

3. Enders Island. You can learn more about Enders Island on the Internet at www.endersisland.com if you wish to visit or make a donation to the retreat center.

3. Getting Started

1. A "skeg" is a very shallow keel on the hull of the boat, usually no more that one to two inches. They can either be retractable or fixed.

2. ConnYak is a Connecticut kayaking group that has a busy paddling schedule for members during the boating months. Their website is www.connyak.org.

3. RICKA is a Rhode Island canoe and kayaking association. Their website is www.ricka.org.

4. The Tuesday Night Paddlers will be described in more detail in a later chapter.

5. Collinsville Canoe and Kakyak Center is near East Hartford. Their website is www.cckstore.com.

6. The Wickford Kayak Center facilities and training courses can be reviewed on their website at www.kayakcentre.com.

7. North Cove Outfitters are located on Main Street, Old Saybrook, Connecticut. Their website is www.northcove.com.

8. REI: "what began as a group of 23 mountain climbing buddies is now the nation's largest consumer cooperative with more than 2.8 million members". Their website is www.rei.com.

4. East To Stonington
    1. "The wind had bundled up the clouds..". An excerpt from *"Red Hanrahan's Song about Ireland"* by W. B. Yeats. Altered to past tense.

5. Tuesday Night Paddlers
    1. The Mystic Times, one of the local broadsheets can be viewed at: http://mystictimes.shorepublishing.com/.

    2. The second broadsheet is the Mystic River Press.

    3. A Tuesday Night Paddlers Schedule is attached in an appendix at the end of this notes section.

    4. The Paddlers website wanders around a little but can usually be found via the RICA site.

7. An Industrious River
    1. Checkout http://www.oceanology.org/ on the Internet for more information on Project Oceanology.

    2. Bryson's comment on thoughtless architecture is from his book *"The Lost Continent"*.

    3. Electric Boat is the submarine division of General Dynamics Corporation.

    4. You can read more about the *"Thresher"* calamity on the National Geographic Web site at: http://www.nationalgeographic.com/k19/disastersdetail2.html.

5. *"The Hunt for Red October"*, the famous submarine thriller and movie by Tom Clancy.

6. "Wooden ways." A "way" is a description of an inclined cradle in which a boat can be built or launched.

8. East Of Stonington
1. *"Sudden Sea: The Great Hurricane of 1938,"* by R.A. Scotti.

9. Dancing In The Dark
"The Wind in the Willows," a timeless river classic by Frederick Graham.

10. Fishers Island
1. *"Plum Island"* by Nelson DeMille. A mystery novel (which I have not read but intend to) combining history, bioresearch and crime.

2. *"Lab 257 : The Disturbing Story of the Government's Secret Plum Island Germ Laboratory,"* By Michael C. Carroll.

11. Further Afield
1. *"Tidewaters of the Connecticut River: An explorer's guide to hidden coves and marshes,"* by Thomas J. Maloney. This is a lovely guide to the lower reaches of the river.

2. "Daggers" are a short open kayak akin to whitewater craft.

3. There is a nuclear power plant at Millstone in Waterford.

4. "Paddling Inn to Inn in Maine", New York Times, July 13' 1997.

The "50'-s" List

1. Posterity. "Why should we put ourselves out of our way to do anything for posterity; for what has posterity done for us? (*Laughter*). I apprehend you gentleman have entirely mistaken my words, I assure the house that by posterity I do not mean my ancestors but those who came immediately after them". Attributed to Irish parliamentarian, Sir Boyle Roche. *"A Little Book of Irish Quotations,"* by Sean McMahon.

Convenient Coastal Access Locations for Kayakers
(compiled from a recent Tuesday Night Paddlers schedule)

Water Access Point	Suggested Destination	Directions To Water Access Point
Barn Island, State Boat Launch, Stonington, Ct	Sandy Point Latimer Light Watch Hill	I-95 to exit 91, Stonington Borough exit, south on North Main street to Rte-1 light. Left on Rte-1, past Cove Side Marina (on right) to light. Right on Greenhaven Road, first right on Palmer Neck Road, 1.5 miles to end at boat ramp.
Bayberry Lane State Boat Launch, Groton Ct	Mumford Cove Thames River	I-95 to Exit 87 to Clarence Sharp Highway. Through two lights on Brandagee to Shenecosstt Road. Past Pfizer & Golf Course, under Amtrak, second left on Bayberry Lane.
Deep River, Ct	Selden Island	I-95 to Rte 9 North. Take Exit 5 and cross Rte-154 to River Street. Proceed to boat launch.
Esker Point Beach, Groton, Ct	Mystic River Groton Long Point Fishers Island	I-95 to Exit 88. South on Rte-117 to end, left at light on Rte-1 to top of hill. Right on Rte-215 to beach on left
Essex, Ct	Essex Harbor Ct River	I-95 to Rte-9 to Exit 3. Go to stop light then east on West Avenue into Essex Center. At the Rotary at the head of Main Street go north (left) on North Main Street for one short block and turn right onto Bushnell Street. Just before Dauntless Boat Yard turn left onto a dirt road and go a short distance to boat launch and parking area.

Fort Wetherill, Jamestown, RI	Newport Harbor	I-95 to Rhode Island. Rte-138 East (Exit 3A). Cross Jamestown Bridge and take Downtown Jamestown exit just before the Newport Bridge tolls on the east side of the island. Follow signs to Fort Wetherill. Turn right into park and take a quick left to the boat launch parking area. Fort Wetherill is on the east side of the island.
Four Mile River Boat Launch, Old Lyme Ct	Pattagansett Marsh	I-95 to Exit 72 (Rocky Neck Connector). South to Rte-156 to stop light. Take right and go to stop sign. Left and follow sign to boat launch on left.
Great Island State Boat Launch, Old Lyme, Ct	Great Island	I-95 to Exit 70, to light. Left at light through Center to Rte-156. Go left and follow signs to State Boat Launch.
Mystic Y (formerly Mystic Community Center, MCC), Mystic, Ct	Mystic River Ram Island Esker Point	I-95 to Exit 90. South on Rte-27 past Mystic Seaport on Greenmanville Ave to Rte-1 light. Left on Rte-1. Next right at light onto Masons Island Road, over bridge to Community Center on Right. Beach is at back.
Ninigret Pond, RI	Ninigret Pond and Charlestown Breachway	Rte-1 North from Westerly RI to Ninigret Park and Pond exit. Third right to dead-end at marina. Put-in is narrow culvert straight ahead.
Peruzotti Groton Town Boat Launch, Groton, Ct	Pine Island Bluff Point Thames River	I-95 to Exit 88. South on Rte-117 to end. Right on Rte-1 to second light, left onto Airport Road. Turn left into Burrows field behind railroad bridge.
Quiambaug Cove, Mystic-Shore Launch,	Masons Island	I-95 exit 90. South on Rte-27 past Mystic Seaport on Greenmanville Ave to Rte-1 light. Left on Rte-1,

ington, Ct	Stonington Harbor	approx two miles past A&P to Wilcox road. Go right and park in immediate car park. Small put-in is across the road.
Small Boat Association Stonington Borough, Stonington, Ct	Quiambaug Cove Sandy Point Watch Hill	I-95 to Exit 91. Follow signs to Stonington Borough (North Main Street) south through light (Rte-1), left on Trumbull Street to end. Right over viaduct (Alpha Avenue) onto Broad Street to Town Dock. Launch near boat storage area.
Thimble Islands, Stony Creek, Ct	Thimble Islands	I-95 to Exit 58. South on Rte-77, cross Rte-1 to Rte-146. West on Rte-146 for 1 mile, pass under the railroad tracks. Go straight onto Sachems Head Road then right onto Trolley Road.
Walkers Dock Stonington, Private Launch Site, Stonington, Ct	Stonington Harbor Latimer Light Quiambaug Cove	I-95 to Exit 91. South on Main Street to Rte-1 light. Left on Rte-1 past Stonington Feed. Hard Right on Rte-1A to fork, bear left on Elm Street to Meadow Lane on left. First left on Islands Road (dead-end) to Walkers Dock.
Waterford Dock Road Boat Access, Waterford, Ct	Waterford Beach Niantic	Southbound I-95 to Exit 81 (Cross Road). (Northbound take I-95 to exit 75 and bear right to Rte-1.) Left at stop sign then left at light and cross over I-95. Left at next light onto Rte-1. Turn right on Avery Lane then straight through next light to Rte-213 (Great Neck Road). Two miles to Goshen Road, turn right. Follow signs to end to boat access.